LIES AND LIMERICKS
INSPIRATIONS FROM IRELAND

Writers House books from TripleTree Publishing:

Word by Word
Pronto! Writings from Rome
Ship's Log: Writings At Sea
Lies and Limericks: Inspirations from Ireland

LIES AND LIMERICKS
INSPIRATIONS FROM IRELAND

Edited by John Tullius

WRITERS
HOUSE
BOOKS

© 2006 TripleTree Publishing

Lies and Limericks: Inspirations from Ireland
ISBN: 0-9716638-9-0

Library of Congress Control Number 2006929381

Introduction © 2006 Elizabeth Engstrom
"Eileen and the Rock" © 2006 Lisa Alber
"The Hanging of Old Al Crotty" © 2006 Terry Brooks
"Lost and Found" © 2006 Dani Brown
"A Promise to Return" © 2006 Stacy Allen
"Angel Aware" © 2006 Ardith Ashton
"Black Pool" © 2006 Carolyn Buchanan
"No Pain, Dairee" © 2006 Elizabeth George
"Pigeons and Crumbs" © 2006 Aimée Carter
"Dublin Time" © 2006 Bonnie Christoffersen
"Handouts and Hangups" © 2006 Lucie Barron Eggleston
"A Letter from Honora" © 2006 Jerry Eiting
"Stone Walls" © 2006 Val Ford
"Reflections of a Retired Black Woman" © 2006 Gail Harris
"The Doors" © 2006 Judith Heath
"Why We Are in Baghdad" © 2006 Christopher Keane
"Out of Time" © 2006 Judith G. Lyeth
"It Ain't Right" © 2006 Mike Malaghan
"Counterpoint on the Streets of Dublin" © 2006 David Nutt
"The Druid Knot" © 2006 Richard Ramsey
"Little Friends In Ireland" © 2006 Myrtle Forberg Siebert
"The Traveler's Wiles" © 2006 Margaret Stratton, Psy.D.
"Sign Language" © 2006 John Tullius
"Faith and Hope" © 2006 Heather Varez
"Hawk's Wings" © 2006 Margaret Zacharias

A Writers House Book
TripleTree Publishing
PO Box 5684, Eugene, OR 97405
(541) 338-3184 – www.TripleTreePub.com

Cover and interior design by Alan M. Clark
Cover photos by Al Cratty
Printed in the United States of America
1 2 3 4 5 6 7 8 9

All royalties from the sale of this book benefit
the Maui Writers Foundation

Table of Contents

Introduction

Ireland is for writers.

James Joyce. C.S. Lewis. William Butler Yeats. George Bernard Shaw. Bram Stoker. Jonathan Swift. Oscar Wilde. Need I go on?

So when the Maui Writers Conference decided to do another off-campus writing retreat/adventure, Ireland was a natural. We'd already plumbed the Caribbean (not a pirate in sight, though, darn it), Alaska and its expansive wonders, and Rome, ancient city full of tales.

And then we set our sights on the emerald jewel.

Ireland.

Ireland is for writers.

Just trying to capture that unmistakable Irish accent on paper would require a lifetime of exercises in writing dialogue. And then there is the misty rain, the green hillsides, innumerable flocks of sheep, narrow winding roads, ruined castles, stunning golf courses, all rich with history peculiar to this spectacular island nation.

And let us not forget leprechauns, faeries and all the rest of the fanciful folk.

There is Dublin, clean, spirited, and alive with its enormous parks and Trinity College, which houses a massive library and the Book of Kells. The population of Dublin is younger than any of us expected, and night time saw the pubs fill up and all that youthful, Guinness-fueled exuberance spilling out into the streets.

Just the texture of Irish linen, or handwoven goods made of the wool from Irish sheep is enough to make one fall in love with the artistry that abounds, whether it be Waterford crystal or the artistic craftsmanship of a thatch roof—ancient and still holding.

The Irish are a solid people with a fierce love of their land. Their history is peppered with tales of war—not over any commodity, but over control of the land. Their livelihood came from the land, and when it failed them, life became even harder, and drew them all closer.

All of this is rich fodder for the fertile imaginations of writers.

Twenty-five of us went to Ireland one May to immerse ourselves in this richness, to be inspired, and to write stories, essays, and even poems, based on those inspirations. Each writer was challenged to write two complete projects during the ten day retreat.

And write we did.

We learned, as writers always do, more about ourselves in the process. We also made new friends, and cemented old friendships over civilized tea, over a pub lunch of Irish stew, as we listened to a haunting "Ave Maria" in an old castle chapel, and while we drove around the Ring of Kerry. We were tourists with an agenda—not just looking and nodding, listening to the tour guide with half our attention—we were rabidly interested in finding the next kernel of intrigue that would lead to a story.

Because writing is such an intense endeavor, we threw in a limerick contest for levity.

In the midst of a discussion over titles, we stopped at a pub for a light lunch and a half pint. We asked the bartender: "What would you call a book full of stories inspired by Ireland?"

"Lies," he said with a twinkle.

And so here they are.

But if Ireland taught me anything, it's something that Joyce, Lewis, Yeats, Shaw, Stoker, Swift, Wilde, and Frank McCourt taught me long ago.

Ireland is for readers.

Enjoy.

   —Elizabeth Engstrom

For me, inspiration often comes from place, and in particular a fascinating fact specific to a setting. I can tell I'm nibbling on a story seed when I find myself jotting notes while, for example, hunched in a doorway during a downpour. Two days earlier, we'd toured a famous archaeological site called the Rock of Cashel, with its fortress walls, round tower, open-air abbey and Romanesque chapel. Though I found the site itself compelling, it wasn't until the tour guide mentioned the Birth Registry of 1930 *that I felt The Grab (as I call it): oh, that's too cool and I must take note. Usually I get a sense for my main characters, then start writing; in this case, I heard the voice of the story instead. In fact, here's the first sentence (complete with bad grammar) that I jotted in my notebook during the downpour, which was the start of my exploration into the omniscient voice: "There's some who knew that old* Birth Registry of 1930 *would cause the Cashel family no end of grief."*

By the way, I did not make up the right to pass Rock of Cashel burial spots down to the next generation; this quirky fact and its inherent potential for conflict was the hook that got me started on "Eileen and the Rock."

EILEEN AND THE ROCK

by Lisa Alber

Some of the lads still insist the stranger caused the Cashel family troubles. With all gathered around to toast the old man's demise and no one the wiser, up he stepped to our host, the new laird of the manor, with a *hello brother; I'm here to claim my place.* Could have been asking for the gents for all the fanfare he spoke, and for all the quiet that spread about the room you'd have thought folks were witnessing the return of the original prodigal son. The hush lasted long enough that all jumped when that vixen Eileen gave a keening wail and flopped to the floor like a rag-stuffed doll.

Down at The Deaf Justice Pub where Alan, now all of 80, still pours a Guinness the likes of none, there's others who blame the American lass, Eileen, for the grief. She a Boston Brahmin, lineage of Butler descent off the Mayflower so she liked to claim, but that was for shite. She was Southie Boston all the way and just the woman to bring down a solid local family.

Or, you could travel back to the *Birth Registry of 1930* for the blame, but that's asking for a kick in the balls around here, that registry being a most fascinating bit of local history. A matter of pride, that's right, and you'll not be blaming a piece of moldering paper for some people's peculiar obsessions.

❧

Eileen, now she was a pretty sort of girl and on the day of old man Cashel's burial back in 1973, she sat demure as a buttercup amongst stinging nettles. She wore a clingy dress with a plunging V-neck, dark as night but hatched through with lighter strands to enhance her eyes—though Alan's the only one to say that; the rest of the locals merely thought as she looked soulful and innocent with her wide blue eyes and comely freckled chest. Her fiancé, Evan Cashel, wore the mandated black and cleared his throat every now and then to prove he struggled against tears, but though some couldn't help noticing that his gaze rarely roamed far from Eileen's peeping cleavage.

This was the season of the flowering laburnum, whose yellow blooms scented the air sweet as harem baths while starlings busied themselves building nests in the chapel's eaves. Eileen, dear girl, missed the beauty of the day, not to mention Father O'Toole's eulogy, because her thoughts tended to gravitate to her two-carat diamond, which was bigger than those of the posh ladies on Beacon Hill and surely her highness Mrs. Benedict would faint to see her maid's daughter now.

From pleasant fantasies of showing-up Mrs. Benedict, Eileen's reveries returned as usual to the Rock of Cashel, where the pagan kings of Munster ruled and archbishops later prayed. Up there atop the hill overlooking the village, you've seen them, the ruins of the medieval cathedral and round tower. Quite the cachet to be buried there, so that Eileen in her wraparound dresses liked to say, and now that the old man was dead—God rest his soul—she was as good as in. She imagined resting in an open casket—mahogany no less— with her face made up to perfection and a tearful procession winding up to the Rock. She'd not be lumped in with the rest of her Southie family, just another O'Leary brat with no future for her but to follow her mother into the servants' entrances of those Beacon Hill mansions and then at the end of a toiling life only have money enough for—heaven help her—cremation. Burnt to a crisp wasn't her way; she desired immortality by way of the ultimate burial plot.

By now, you're wondering why mere dirt held such *cachet*, as it were. This is where the *Burial Registry of 1930* enters the tale. In that fateful year the grounds around the old cathedral were closed to further burials except for certain local and living families of the time, which is to say the O'Tooles and the Shaunessys; the Finns and the McNamaras; not to mention the oldest clan of all, the Cashels. The precious dirt allotments passed on to the next generation if unused, and as old man Cashel preferred to be buried alongside his drinking mates, the rights to burial passed over the old man's son, who died of the drink at too young an age, and on to grandson Evan. Theirs was the last unused spot up at the Rock, which, of course, added to its *cachet*.

Old man Cashel was a tugboat of a man, wide as he was tall, always fat truth be told, and those kind purveyors of dirt back in 1930 were smart enough to predict he'd grow nothing but bigger as time passed. You might be saying that it was the old man's morbid obesity that caught Evan his fair Eileen. Canny, she was, and in the way of women who instantly size up dresses on hangers, she knew there'd be space enough to fit herself in beside Evan up at the Rock. That girl set herself upon Evan and poor bloody sod with a wart for a brain knew nothing but bliss at her hands—literally, for she was demure by appearance only.

❧

There's some that claim they noticed the stranger in their

midst that day, but could be the whiskey talking for all that, Alan having held a pre-funeral wake at the pub for those as considered the old man their mate in the pints. Regardless whether or not they noticed at the time, there *was* a stranger yonder by baby Finn's grave marker, standing still as a sentinel next to the limestone angel. Irish, to be sure, but not local. Not an O'Toole or a Shaunessy, not a Finn or a McNamara. He wore his hat the proper way of the Dubliner and leaned against the angel with the nonchalance of, God help us all, a Prod.

Eileen, that minx, noticed him straight away and imagined lashing him up to the canopied bed soon to reside in her private bedroom suite. Looked to be packing a sporting rod in his trousers, so she observed, and looked to be a working man at that. She sniffed with remorse that brought on the sympathy from more than one spectator, all the while her thinking she'd be hard-pressed to rid herself of her old desires: those wild Southie lads with their roughened hands and untidy manners. She clenched her thighs together rather than feel them quiver at the thought of well-worked muscles on lean bodies, none of these cream-fatted hairless expanses as sported by her dear Evan.

So it was that during old man Cashel's internment pretty Eileen fantasized her way through the eulogy and managed to endear herself to everyone all the more for her chastely pressed legs. Afterwards, Evan with his Eileen led the way along narrow lanes to the family manor. Evan, for his part, found death tedious business, but with Eileen on his arm he strolled along willingly enough, nodding at the passing comment made by his beloved about their wedding colors, cerise and silver.

"It will be lovely," said she, "yet original. We'll find the perfect altar cloth, which won't be too ostentatious, nor too modest. Speaking of which, I was thinking of the McNamara's plot up at the Rock. I took a turn the other day you know, mourning our poor grandfather, and I walked past the McNamara's spot without remarking it."

"Hmm?"

Evan wondered if the cook had fixed up his favorite chops with mint. Surely she'd know to prepare the meal the same as any Wednesday despite the guests and the buffet table. There'd be nothing but bits and pieces for nibbling otherwise, which never suited him.

"And it seemed to me," said Eileen with the special voice she kept for Evan. She practiced an hour each day in the privacy of her boudoir: a sing-song cadence low and sweet as a lullaby, void of pretense, filled with promised pleasures, all sure to mesmerize Evan to her way of thinking. "It seemed to me," said she, "shocking that such a prominent family has no stone to speak of. Why, they're as important to local history as anyone!"

"Right," Evan said and pressed a hand against his grumbling stomach.

"Oh I agree," said she, "it's not right, and I can't help but feel sad that our poor grandfather has nothing for himself there either."

"Hmm?"

"Such an astute man, you get my meaning exactly. We'll need to commission a sculpture for his spot. I've designed it in my head already. *Cashel* across the top with the doves he loved to shoot all around the name. Everyone knows what a good shot he was in his day."

"Sounds grand," Evan said.

"Oh I agree; and how grand that we came up with the idea!"

"Spot on," he said and squeezed her arm, thinking her too perfect to know his mind before he did.

As they walked on, his thoughts returned to food and hers to the intricacies of grave marker design. She pictured a tall monument with plenty of space on the lower majority to fit Evan's name and her own, plus modest but charming blessings perfect for tourist rubbings. Her name would then live on through the tour guides' fond stories. She sighed and leaned against Evan's arm, and all following thought how touching that she felt the emotion of the day so keenly.

All, that is, except the stranger. He kept to himself quiet

as a nun's bed until an hour later when confronted with 20-foot ceilings, Irish oak banisters, mullioned windows, and gold-leafing throughout. "So this is the family seat," he said, and Alan later claimed to notice a tone to his voice, a curiosity with too much pride of place to be appropriate.

♣

Now skip forward to the moment of quiet within the manor's drawing room. Eileen, for all her sham, fainted honestly enough to hear of a new Cashel brother. No one knew what to do, caught as they were between helping her and rushing the stranger, who finally announced his name was Gabriel, rightful heir to the seat.

"Hold now," Evan said, "I'm thinking."

As said earlier: a wart for a brain, poor sod. While Evan pulled on his lower lip, the fair Eileen's eyelids fluttered. She flipped a hand to be sure of the diamond, remembered the birth registry, and pushed herself to her feet with the fluid movement of a woman with an agenda. She slipped in next to Evan and fashioned herself a winsome smile. "I'm sorry, you are?"

"Gabriel."

"I'm sure we can straighten out this misunderstanding; meanwhile, please enjoy yourself for as long as you like."

Now Gabriel, he was no fool. In an instant he knew Eileen for one step above the shady ladies who took him in after he fled the nuns. Those good whores were the ones to recognize him for genteel blooded. They insisted he seek out his birthright, that they did, and they taught him the finer points of self-preservation, not to mention a certain kind of scrappiness. Gabriel, he wasn't a bad man, only one who had long ago wearied of the gritty side of life, especially after so many years spent tracking down his bloodline (and a fine tale this is for the future telling).

"On second thought," Eileen continued with a wrinkle to her nose, "perhaps you'd like a shower before joining us?"

"Excuse me," Evan said, listening to his grumbling insides instead of his sweetheart. "I'll check on my meal." The truth was, he couldn't think on an empty stomach, not that

14

food improved his processing, but never you mind: he was the kindliest man you'd ever want to meet.

Meanwhile, in response to Eileen's jibe, Gabriel wandered through the mob that stood transfixed stupid as puppets on strings.

What could the man be about? had to be going through a fair number of minds by then because Gabriel sauntered clear over to the other side of the room. That stately manor house—now part of the Irish national heritage and open to the public—sported an Italian marble fireplace big enough to spit a sheep. Gabriel parked himself behind one of the armchairs in front of said fireplace and arranged himself in a pose that looked to be straight out of a magazine for staid country living, with one ankle crossed in front of the other, hand in pocket and jacket slung behind his hip. A cocky kind of pose with his chin straight to the horizon.

"What the hell?" Alan muttered, and his wife—God bless her soul—hushed him sure enough, busy as she was memorizing details for the pub gossips.

If pretty Eileen still ogled Gabriel's rod there's no way of knowing because just that moment a crash of Wedgwood China sounded from the back of the room and Evan was heard to yell, "Christ almighty, will you look at that?"

What, what? came the chorus except for Eileen who caught on quick enough when she spied Evan's darting glances between Gabriel and the wall above the carved mantel. "You're the bloody image of him," Evan yelled. "Brother!"

Indeed! There stood Gabriel in mimic of a portrait, circa 1920, of right honorable old man Cashel in the prime of life with jodhpurs and riding boots, ankles crossed just so, arm cocked, profile jutting. Despite the watch fob, high-starched collar, and handlebar moustache, you'd not be mistaking Gabriel for any but the old man's grandson. Some remarked later that the resemblance wasn't obvious at first because Gabriel was thin to the old man's fat but that the muttonchop sideburns turned the corner for them, this being the 1970s and Gabriel coming direct from Dublin, height of fashion he was by their parochial reckoning. Thick facial fur identical to the old man, no one could deny it, not even fair Eileen, who stood with her mouth agape before recollecting herself.

"Evan, darling," said she, "I'm still feeling faint; could you fetch me water, please?"

"Of course."

Gabriel cast an eyebrow in his newfound brother's direction but said nothing. He wasn't likely to at that point because he knew the lay of the land. Eileen, so he'd heard, enjoyed her way well enough, and her way was mistress of the manor with its all-important Rock of Cashel perk. Despite his bloodline, Gabriel knew himself to be on shaky ground. For a moment, he wondered whether to follow his brother or stay with the fiancée. Quick-witted devil that he was—the social calculation made in the blink of an eye—he said with purpose, "You stay with your pretty wife, Brother, while I bring the water."

Despite herself, Eileen felt a blush rise. *Wife.* That most perfect of words. Gabriel felt her further measure in the instant even as Eileen caught herself again and aimed a suspicious glance at him. More than suspicious, hers was an eyeful of glint sharp enough to scare a lesser man than Gabriel. Meanwhile, poor Evan beckoned the maid to never mind the pork chop mess on the floor and run fetch another helping.

By the time Gabriel returned with the water, the family solicitor who was a Shaunessey huddled with Evan off in a corner. He'd pulled a mass of papers from his briefcase, and those who had a mind to pretended at perusing hunting scenes along the walls near enough to eavesdrop on their conversation. Later, all at The Deaf Justice agreed that unlike logic might dictate, Evan begged the solicitor to find a loophole for Gabriel. Alan insists he heard the word *loophole* then Shaunessy's response that he happened to carry just such a document. And Christ, but for the first time in his simple life Evan felt decisive and certain. Poor Evan never liked being an only child, and on this day he almost cheered down the stone walls he was that joyful to have a brother, an older one at that, and a man of such obvious intellect to oversee the wretched financials that came along with the Cashel name.

Eileen watched her beloved with rising fear. She felt Evan's energy buoyant as a puppy and knew her place up at the Rock as good as gone to Gabriel if she couldn't guide her dim-witted love along the only correct path to their shared happiness. Gabriel must go. Nothing but a bastard son, after all, born of trash Christ only knew from which farmer's family.

"Forgetting your water?" Gabriel said then, and was that a knowing slight of eye in her direction? "Ay-well," he continued while Eileen tried not to mind his working-man's hands and the way their palms cupped the glass. "I was that sad to learn both my mother and father are beneath the ground—but finding a brother is the saving grace."

"The same mother too?" she said. "I find that hard to believe."

"What can I say but that unwed pregnancy was as taboo for a couple in love as not. They were too young to marry, so off I went to the nuns, all very hush-hush of course. I'm this glad my parents married in the end. Seems they even came to fetch me, but by then I was long gone."

Eileen felt faint. Gabriel, the heir apparent; not some bastard, but a full brother to her Evan, who was just then waving a codicil like he'd won the bloody pot of gold. "Holy hell, it's all here left in my own grandfather's writing!"

There's some who swear Eileen lost her polish then. Was that a most unbecoming curl of lip? The beginning of a snarl low in her throat? Alan swears it's so and that he began to wonder about the fair Eileen the moment she grabbed the handwritten addendum from the solicitor Shaunessy with not a *please* or a *thank you*, not even a simper or a coy blink.

While Evan pulled Gabriel into a hug to embarrass the good Father O'Toole, Eileen read the following words and profound words they were:

> *As my son went the way of the dodo before me, I*
> *add this addendum to my last will and testament that*

his dying wish be granted. Namely, that if his oldest son who was left to the nuns with the name Gabriel ever be found, he be considered patriarch after me with the responsibilities and rewards this entails, which shall include ownership of Cashel Manor and lands, hostelries along the west coast and other business ventures, and burial rights at the Rock of Cashel. (At this, Eileen blanched white as curdled milk.) *Evan as second son shall always have rights to life in the manor, a generous living, and an appropriate position within the family businesses.*

You could have thrown out the whiskey and still called the wake brilliant the surprise that spread through the room. Old man Cashel, fair-minded and generous indeed! And no one the happier than wart-for-brain Evan who fairly skipped around the parlor calling out for champagne.

This could be a corseted story written by that randy bastard Oscar Wilde the way the entailment went down, yet so it was that even in post-war, post-independent Ireland the Cashels maintained the tradition of oldest son as heir. And dearest Eileen with no say in the matter, poor thing.

She let Evan's unseemly joy peter out on its own—it wouldn't do to appear churlish after all—and when he finally stood over the back of an armchair panting for a refill of chops with mint, she tucked an arm around his elbow and whispered into his ear.

Around the couple, guests toasted Gabriel, and Alan himself pulled out a fiddle. Gabriel let himself be feted while keeping gimlet glance on his almost sister-in-law. You might be asking what he thought of her now that he knew his position solid within the family. Why, he shouldn't have minded her influence over Evan now, perhaps even looked on their relationship with amused condescension, he having long ago lost all romantic notions about the fairer sex. Alas and however, he did mind her influence, her wiles, her provocative chest heaves, and most of all, her continued presence in his new home. He'd lived with enough tarts in his gritty days, and he could stomach no more. Simply put, he considered himself a lifelong bachelor with no needs except the shag on the sly. That he'd already pondered buxom Eileen for such a tumble goes without saying—a tart was a tart, after all—but to live with her? Now there was a potential hell worse than the nuns ever lashed into him.

While Gabriel sipped his champagne and imagined a ride on the fair Eileen before tossing her to the glue farm called the curb, that Eileen, she continued whispering into her beloved's ear.

"Oh, I agree, it's wonderful," said she, "but our grandfather forgot to be fair."

The chops with mint arrived and Evan tucked in with the alacrity of the starved. You'd have thought he'd gone without when in fact the remains of the first chop glistened on his chin. "Hmm?" he said. "I don't follow."

"You're just humoring me now, you wretch," said she and reminded herself to put the lullaby into her voice despite her frayed nerves. "You darling wretch of a man, I know you get my meaning that something's owed you for seeing grandfather through his illness."

"Well," Evan said.

"*Well* is right," said she. "It's your deep well of filial duty that saw his last days peaceful." She resisted the urge to wipe meat juice off her darling's face and continued, "Why even a token to show his gratitude."

"Token?"

"Like the tokens of love you give me each day," said she, all the while aiming her glint at Gabriel, who raised his glass toward her with a wink—how dare he? What could the horrid man possibly mean by that? Though deep down she knew his thoughts well enough, and indeed she did, for Gabriel just then decided that the sooner he cut Evan's cord to her joyful mound, the better for them all. Fair Eileen who knew the value of the female genitalia battled her vocal cords to remain sonorous into her beloved's ear even as she absorbed—and enjoyed, don't you be doubting it—Gabriel's lingering stare at her breasts. Outrageous man.

"A token, that's all," said she. "No need to be greedy, after all. You and I, we have simple needs. A roof over our heads."

"Which we still have," Evan said, complacent with pork and unheeding of the gristle stuck between his teeth.

"Indeed," said she, "and we're the lucky ones. We have all we need to enjoy our living days." She heaved a breath as much in disgust at her beloved's continued chewing like a cow at her cud as to cause her pert breasts to inflate against his arm. "But I fear for our dying days."

Evan grunted a question mark.

"Gabriel can't be attached to the Rock," said she. "Not like you are, and besides, the two of you will never fit side by side in the plot. Our grandfather surely meant to leave his burial spot to you as his token."

"Ah right, the token."

His tone remained puzzled and Eileen pushed her breast more firmly against his arm. "You see my meaning as usual— how I love you. You and I shall nestle side by side into eternity with the tour guides to tell our love story. Why, our grandfather said so on his last day, you know, he was that fond of me. Poor man, he was too sick to change his will."

"Too sick, indeed he was." Evan slurped on bone strong enough to suction out the marrow. A minute later he said, "Oh, I follow."

"Of course you do," said she. "No doubt Gabriel will heed our grandfather's intent even if it's not in writing. At least I hope so."

"Well, why not? He seems a jolly fellow, but."

Hello, what's this? A *but* coming just as she felt relief like the last breath before sleep? Never had Evan *but*ted his dear Eileen, never had he seen fit to muster an independent thought while she whispered in his ear. Her previous fear turned to desperation at this oddity, and she blamed the interloper Gabriel who now tossed back a jig of whiskey and made merry with *her* locals. Look at him carrying on with them, quite in league as it were, and why should she be surprised what with his working-man's hands and atrocious manners to go along with his too-tight trousers. Imagine, introducing himself at our grandfather's wake; how gauche.

While Eileen's thoughts ran amuck, Evan considered the state of his stomach and decided another helping of chops with mint would not be amiss, this being a celebration and all.

♣

Hold now, here's the pause required because Alan always calls attention to this turning point for the family Cashel. Most of the lads argue against him, but Alan works with a few brain cells even now and 'tis true that this was the moment of reckoning. Nothing momentous, mind you, just bits and pieces that went missing or astray, that if not, could have seen the family fertile to this day.

What went missing was a thought or two on Eileen's part. She that is canny was so lost in growing anger (self-righteous at that) that she missed the chance to hear her beloved out. Instead, she took that lingering *but* as a personal affront and huffed to the closest bathroom to throw a silent tantrum.

As for the wart-for-brain, if not for his cravings, he'd have finished the thought *but I wouldn't want to hurt Gabriel's feelings*. Meaning he was on task to ask fair Eileen's advice on how best to approach his brother about relinquishing the burial rights. Evan's thoughts strayed often enough, too true, but sometimes they returned. Only now, with his fiancée not there to help him along, as Alan says, all was lost.

If only fair Eileen had heard her beloved through, if only Evan had thereafter broached the topic with Gabriel, why it's some that say Gabriel was tempted to turn his attitude around. They'd be calling correct on that score because the moment Evan called for yet more chop with mint, Gabriel felt within himself a welling solicitude toward his younger brother, a paternalism that took him by surprise. Look at the wanker with drippings on his tie: he deserved his happiness. Gabriel cared nothing for a patch of soil within a tourist attraction and witnessing the weepy love in Evan's eyes for his Eileen nearly thawed Gabriel's heart enough to allow her respite—though in the opposite wing as he, of course. Alas, the potential melt iced over again when Gabriel observed Eileen's parting shot of anger, not to mention disgust, aimed at her beloved. He grinned to himself as he threw back another shot. Got you now, he thought.

❧

There's nothing so grim as a woman who dares not scream, and Eileen in the bathroom was a sight to cause nightmares. She stomped back and forth on the area rug with fists waving in the air and mouth yawning open like that famous painting. Her neck tendons stood in relief and sweat (yes!) glistened on her brow, and when she finished, she stood heaving those lovely breasts in true agitation. For several minutes, she concentrated on her diamond. She let its refracting wink calm her back to her Southie street-wise roots. Why, the solution was obvious, that classic female strategy: nothing more than goodnight kisses for Evan until he saw the error of his *but*.

Back in the parlor with the festivities reaching a pitch to shatter glass, Gabriel lounged with his brother. They made quite the picture, Gabriel and Evan, sitting with knees spread and whiskeys in hand, both with the sturdy Cashel jaw, the one firm, the other slack, but the same nonetheless. "What say you?" Gabriel said. "I take it we're square?"

"You're feckin' straight we're square. This is the best feckin' day of my life!"

"Good, good."

"Only Eileen seems a bit put out, she does." Evan shrugged. "Must be the stress of the day. She'll be fine given a moment."

Gabriel had his doubts, which were confirmed two seconds later when Eileen regained the room. She flashed a smile at Alan that further gathered the tension around her jaw. "Play on," she called with a tad too much shrill for anyone's liking.

Gabriel noted the red leaking from her cheeks when she caught sight of them cozy on the couch, which was a tableau he had orchestrated especially for her. That scrappiest of fellows had also called for yet another chop with mint so that

Evan sat there with yet more dribblings on his face and front, not to mention with his suit jacket open to reveal straining trousers—and not in the arousing way as Eileen was sure to observe. In short, Gabriel read dearest Eileen's switch of allegiance clear as if she'd straddled him with her wraparound dress hiked to the heavens.

❧

Mark this as the truth: Gabriel hastened along what Eileen was soon to decide on her own anyhow. For her, it wasn't much of a jump from withholding sex to tossing Evan away all together. Where everyone else in the room remarked on the brothers's similarities, Eileen—she that is fastidious and dainty—convulsed at their differences. Why, that must be her beloved's, rather *ex*-beloved's, fourth chop with mint, and he with his shiny face and his suit all but ruined and his slack stomach near to popping off his trouser button. Clear as the best Guinness is dark, Eileen realized there would be no controlling Evan. The wart was doomed to follow in his grandfather's obese footsteps. By the time they reached old age she'd be squeezed out of her place up at the Rock by 150 pounds of excess lard.

Gabriel, on the other hand, lounged weedy as a hawthorn branch. She sized him up and found him the better for his boniness. Even allowing for an extra 20, or 30, pounds, there'd still be space enough for her up at the Rock. In her imagination *Evan* disappeared off the grave marker to be replaced by *Gabriel*. Yes, Gabriel, who sat lean and tidy as a dandy of old, clearly the master of his impulses, whether keeping them in line (food) or giving way to them (sex). She shivered, and it was this tremble that Gabriel caught from across the room. Right into his trap she came with hips a-sway and lips a-shine to settle between the brothers Cashel. "My two favorite men," said she. Her hand brushed Gabriel's thigh before settling on her own. The way he then positioned his bulge in her direction, why, she as good as had him seduced with Evan none the wiser. If Mrs. Benedict on Beacon Hill could see her now, the most popular girl to rival Scarlett O'Hara!

"Grand, grand," Evan mumbled between chews. "I knew you'd come around. Lovely, really. And Gabriel here just agreed to walk you down the aisle."

Gabriel tickled her ear with his breath. "With my heartiest congratulations."

He cradled her hand in both of his and lifted it to his lips so slowly dear Eileen felt the melting between her thighs.

"Evan, darling," said she, "you might want to change now that you've got half a pig down your front."

She noticed neither the greasy kiss that landed on her cheek nor his response—*so good of you to notice; I'll do just that*—as her every sense converged on the press of her you-know-whats against Gabriel, who shifted closer with arm snaked along the couch cushion behind her.

"I must apologize for my earlier behavior," he said. "Defensive, I suppose, that ready to be tossed out on my ass."

His candor charmed her as did the way his fingers teased the back of her neck. She imagined the ring he'd gift her when she landed him gulping as a trout on the line. Not a silly emerald-cut, which didn't contain nearly enough facets to shine light off in all directions. How could she have thought her ring superior when the classic round solitaire best showed a diamond's brilliance?

"No matter," said she, "but my, what a shock, your appearance, though pleasant in the end." The perfect pause. "As I'm sure you can tell."

"Indeed," he said, and spied her erect nipples as proof. "It's too bad—"

"Yes?"

"Oh that, well—I suppose we'll need to discuss what you want from me." His pause rivaled hers for perfection. "During the wedding ceremony, that is."

"Gracious, so many details to a wedding. We should confirm how you're to lay me down—rather, walk me down—the aisle."

They agreed on the hour for a *tête-a-tête* over tea. Eileen suggested old man Cashel's library on the other side of the manor, which, conveniently enough, contained a custom-made double-wide sofa and an inside lock.

If you're picturing pretty Eileen a-straddle with her A-line skirt lifted, you'd be correct. Fast forward six hours into the evening with whiskey circulating and bawdy songs raised to the roof—the place was a drunken catastrophe by then—and you'd have witnessed that Eileen plying enough wares to make Gabriel's whore-moms proud.

Gabriel settled her on his lap snug enough, only too willing to grab his shag on the sly. However, was that a tinge of regret shadowing his eyes? No, nothing but a wince as he adjusted his girth for an easier ride. He eyed the grandfather clock over Eileen's shoulder and grinned as she threw back her head with well-done groans of delight. She wasn't anywhere near to coming, and he for one didn't care because he had a timetable to keep. He hurried himself along until the world exploded and a satisfying limpness overtook him.

And just in time, Alan always adds when every bloke in The Deaf Justice sighs over the wondrous shudder that comes with the shag on the sly. Three, two, one, on the dot of 8:30 poor Evan burst into the room, Gabriel having previously unlocked the door while Eileen peeled off her panty hose. "Thank Christ you had Shaunessy remind me to come along for a chat. I'm drunker than a—hmm—can't think of it now."

Any man with brains enough to fart would have sussed out the situation straight away. But not Evan, no. Not to ping too dearly on the wart, but how could he not interpret his Eileen's bare buttocks for anything but *coitus interruptus*?

"Huh?" he said. "What the—?"

To hasten Evan's brain cells along, Gabriel made haste to push Eileen off his lap. "Can't you leave a man alone?" he said with a perfect cry of remorse and regret. "Why, she's just using us, Brother!"

"Huh?" said she. "What the—?"

Fair Eileen, reduced to the stupidity of her fiancé. Her hanging jaw 'twas a sight to behold, that it was. Gabriel would have laughed if he weren't studying Evan's confusion, then denial, then hurt—then, thank Christ, outrage.

After awhile even Evan couldn't mistake Eileen's sticky sprawl upon the oak floorboards.

You can imagine the rest: accusations, denials; insults, sweet nothings; rejection, tearful negotiations; and in the end, Gabriel and Evan, the closest of bachelor brothers to the end of their short-lived days. If Evan appeared sad at times, no one commented; if Gabriel, bitter, likewise. And if Evan never caught on that Gabriel played him for a dupe—for himself *coitus completus* after all—then no matter because he only meant to liberate his brother from that seductress Eileen.

Three husbands later, it's said about Eileen, and with a solitaire the size of a sheep's ball at that. It might be she's the one in the fox fur that visits the Rock now that the brothers have passed on—the one from syphilis caught during his gritty days, the other from blocked arteries. She of the fox fur, who's been heard to mutter *impossible, how did they fit?* while pulling a tape measure out of her purse.

Down at The Deaf Justice, Alan still wonders aloud what might have become of the Cashel family had Evan landed himself a kind-hearted and homely lass, the type with modesty to bring home to ma and servility to bring home to da. Some argue that Gabriel would have tolerated such a piece of furniture and Evan happily married might have swayed him toward ritualized monogamy himself. And then who knows? To this day, you might be seeing family heirs around the village rather than two brothers laid out side by side up at the Rock of Cashel.

*High on a limestone hill that commands the view of pastures
and the town of Cashel rests the ruins of Cashel Castle. At the
heart of the mound is the Cross of St. Patrick and the ruined remains of the enormous church that once stood tall against the sky.
Near the cross, a massive corner of the cathedral wall was ripped
from its origin and now embeds itself, edge first, into the turf.*

THE DRUID KNOT

by Richard Ramsey

A pair of black shadows vaulted over the tall stone wall.
In the clouded night they landed on the inside of the ancient
enclosed grounds. Cashel Castle's walls had been breached.
They looked back at the thirty-hand-high barrier and
shrugged, then hunched close to the ground. Their hooded
forms moved like badgers; looking, sniffing, edging for any
movement that showed they had been discovered. Only the
slight breeze rustling the leaves of the nearby cork oaks made
any mention of the two's arrival.

They gathered their black cloaks and made their way to
the timeworn broken stone of St. Patrick's Cross high on the
grassy hill. One went right, the other left. They searched the
turf and gravel ground. Their hands, palms down, wove over
the ground before them in search of a relic.

The taller of the two said, "I'll check the backside of the
building, over by the gravestones."

"I didn't place it there; it should be here, near the cross."

He stopped and turned to consider her words. She had
been wrong before, not often, but still she could be wrong
again.

He moved against the breeze, letting his robe billow behind like a wraith. The moon peeked through a slit between
the clouds, but still could not light the form that raced around
the backside of the inner broken walls of Cashel Castle. He
sniffed the air and then dove behind a large headstone, his
hands already working over the ground.

He checked the area, then pulled a dagger from under his robe and examined it carefully. He turned the gleaming thin blade in his hand and rotated the silvered handle to guide the edge back into the sheath at his waist.

Moments later he was back. "Are you sure you know the spot?" he asked with irritation.

The woman pulled her black hood back. Her red hair tumbled out of the cowl and off her shoulders as she stared down her partner. High cheekbones and tan freckles defined her face. "If I knew the precise spot, Liam, don't you think I would walk directly to it and be done and done?"

Liam didn't like being assigned to the Preservers. He had worked with them before, but his latest crime was such that he had either community service to perform or sit in a room and listen to oral druidic histories. Neither penalty for his crime was preferred, but sitting in musty hall with a droning monotone elder was the worse of the lot. He smiled as he remembered that this sentence was far less than it should have been. He had people in places that *liked* his work.

The wind blew and brought a light rain. Liam pulled his own hood back to feel the elements on his face. The deep scar across his right cheek funneled most of the rain into a small river to careen down his neck and onto his pale linen tunic. *Much better than the old scriptorium,* he thought. He liked to be out in the fresh air. He liked to be out and free.

The woman searched St. Patrick's Cross for a sign. "I remember placing it around here somewhere. But I don't recall exactly where. The cross looks different, it now only has three arms instead of four. A lot looks different than when I placed the knot."

Liam sat on the rough stone steps of the cross to watch and listen. The castle was not open as yet. The cars, buses and tourists; the ignorant tourists with their noisy children, popcorn, and sticky fingers, would not arrive for some time. He continued to sniff the air occasionally to check, in case he was wrong. He was not about to be caught unaware.

"Kerri, how'd you lose the map?" he asked.

"I didn't do it on purpose. I just misplaced it."

"You misplaced it? The map is the only way to find the failing knot."

Kerri ran her fingers across the rough surface of the broken stone cross. "I know, I know. You don't have to tell me. I've done this before."

His glare bored holes through her lithe form. "You've lost knot maps before?"

"No, not lost, not even misplaced. I mean I've lead missions before to replace failing knots. The map is pretty good in helping to find them, even after thirty-five hundred years, unless the locals uncover it and put it in one of their museums. Then it gets a bit more interesting."

Liam's arms went rigid. He bit his tongue. "A bit more interesting? I almost got caught in one of those museums last year when a guard popped his head out of a closet." Liam thought he would have to kill the guard, until the man fainted at the sight of a black cloaked figure rushing toward him.

Kerri crushed her eyebrows together. "Don't you be telling me about my duties and responsibilities, Liam Donnal McKacey, I wasn't the one who ripped the door off the Treorai's chambers because it was locked. I wasn't the one who nipped the tips of an Elf's ears to make him look more like us. I wasn't the one who pulled the wings off a fairy just to see if they would grow back."

"The elf and fairy were a long time ago, I was quite young. The elf lived and the fairy did grow her wings back, eventually."

He didn't flinch. He ran his fingers down the sheath of the knife attached to his belt. But what he kept to himself was that lately he had also killed two men. The Treorai, head of the Druid Counsil, had ordered him to dispatch the men because of one losing a knot and the other for losing a map. He did not rip the door off the chambers because it was locked. He lost his temper when he was ordered to kill, yet again. He did not like to kill, but he was good at it. He kept those small memories and his true reason for coming to himself. Liam put his hand to the haft of his dagger.

Kerri moved to a large section of wall that had broken off the corner of the cathedral, impelling its cornered edge into the ground.

"Liam, come see this. This isn't right."

Liam pulled his black robe around himself and moved to where Kerri stood at one end of the embedded section of wall. He touched the rock and mortar with a gentle stroking to discern the origin of the piece and the reason of its failure. He felt the rough age of the stone and the mortar that bound it. He could sense the storm that arrived much worse than the present irritating drizzle. The substance of the event rolled out to his mind. For centuries the storm, wind and rain pounded the stone off and on with relentless ferocity until the gale of a fortnight past brought with it lightning. The strike that split the massive piece from its place allowed the heap of stone to tumble, to embed itself in the ground where they stood. Liam jerked his hands back from the weight of the thoughts and strength of the strike that severed the stone from its origin. He felt snapping of invisible strings, as if the lines holding a tent upright had been cut. He opened and closed his hands to push life back into his numb fingers.

"Are you alright?" Kerri reached for Liam.

He jerked away from her as well. "Yes, it was nothing."

"Did you feel anything, anything at all?"

"I felt the stone fall, and land here. I felt strings break. I felt nothing of consequence."

"Strings break?" She appeared to trail off in thought.

Liam kept rubbing his hands.

Kerri pushed a troublesome strand of red hair behind one ear. "I bet the corner of the wall came down and broke the knot. I bet this is where the knot is and why it failed long before it was supposed to. I think I've found the place."

"You think?" He did not know how much more of her excuses he could take. It would be easy to kill her and tell the Treorai that she was unable to find the knot. It would be simple to cut the search short and retrieve his payment. The sun was about to rise and that would be the end of their search. They had to find and replace the knot before sunrise, else the fabric of the fairy veil would be torn further and thus possibly allowing the world for fairy to spill into the world of men. He and Kerri might even be trapped in this world if this was the pivotal knot that released the veil forever.

But wait, was it all that bad? He wouldn't have to do the Treorai's bidding, or killing. He would be free to follow his own path and not that forced on him because of his birth. The curse was being born to druids. His parents made the choice, coming from the men side of the veil to join the assembly in fairy; they considered it a high privilege to be chosen by the fairy for this work. But he was not given any alternative, any choice. He had merely been born.

Liam paced. He wasn't sure that allowing the veil to falter was all that bad. Orcs, dragons, and elves were what he had always known. They were not to be feared, but men don't trust what they don't understand. There would be war, just as before. A war between the fairy and men was what caused the fairy to forge the veil, four millennia in the past. The war might start again, but he didn't care, he might be free of the druids if it did.

"Lift the stone, Liam. Lift it so I can search underneath."

Kerri's request broke into Liam's thoughts and brought him back to the wet that ran down his face, the mud that splashed on his boots, and the voice of a woman a century his junior.

"You know we aren't allowed to use that type of magic in this world. It's not permitted. What are you trying to do, get me in further trouble? Cause me to be putting in more time with you Preservers?"

"I don't see another way. I need to have you lift the stone so I can search beneath. If you don't lift it, I can't find and replace the knot. I don't need to tell you what that would mean."

"You can't discern its location through the stone?"

"No. It seems that the knot may have been broken which caused a guarding of itself to take place. Your sensing the break of the strings of the veil is my only clue." She wiped the rain from her face and pushed her red hair back over her shoulders.

He had to pretend. "I don't like it. I don't like it a bit." He needed to dislike her request, but then again this would be a good time to dispatch her and be done with the issue. Her body would be flat under the weight of the stone. He would not need to dispose of her since the stone would push her corpse beneath his feet. Clean and efficient, that's why the Treorai liked his work.

Liam stood back from the stone and mortar. He raised his hands as if to quiet the steady drizzle, but instead silver-blue particles erupted from his hands and flew to encase the section of wall, stone, and mortar. He moved his fingers to feel the size and weight of the stone, the coarseness of its surface. He needed to find the sweet spot, the point that would allow him to lift it. His magic penetrated the mass of stones. It dove down into the depth, through the rock and mortar to the center of the massive piece. Down his magic ran, down to the crevice of balance.

It was harder than he expected. There was more buried underground than it appeared. He struggled to send his magic within the mass without using all of his reserves at once. The wall shook.

"More, Laim, more. You almost have it."

"Don't be telling me how to lift a stone." He brought his little fingers, the fingers of control, closer to his others and the stream of magic increased. The mass shook and lifted an inch.

"That's not enough."

"Why, are you getting fat?" He retorted. He considered that if he killed her with the stone, he would also not have to listen to her chiding remarks.

He poured more magic into his effort and the stone lifted several feet into the air. "I trust that is enough?"

She smiled and then removed her robe and crawled under the massive rock in her pale linen blouse and ankle-length skirt.

Now was the time for which he had waited. Now was

the time he was to be paid. She would never find the knot, there was no way without a map. No one had ever found a knot without a map. He raised the mass a foot higher. At least he wanted to make sure that she died quickly. He figured he owed her that much. He raised it another foot for good measure.

"I found it," she said.

The stone dropped two feet with the loss of his concentration. Liam opened his control and increased the magic again to stop the stone.

"I found it Liam, I found it," she sang.

"Good, now get out."

What was he saying? This was what he wanted. Kill the girl and claim the payment. Kill the girl and the veil might break forever. Kill the girl and be done with the Treorai ordering him to kill more. What was he thinking? How could he let her live? But, how could he let the only person to find a knot without a map die? How could he kill his cousin, a family connection that not even the Treorai knew about?

"Hurry Kerri, I can't hold it," he said. Sweat beaded on his forehead, his hands shook from the strain.

She scurried back out from under the mass of stone and mortar. Her blue eyes were bright and her smile was as wide as the sun that was just poking above the horizon.

"Slowly lower the stone," she begged. "I placed the knot where I found this broken one."

Liam eased the stone back into place and fell to his knees, panting. The air was cooling to his exhaustion and heat. No one would know what had been done, none but the Druid Counsel and themselves.

Kerri pushed the gravel back up against the mass. She held out her muddy hands to Liam. The broken white gold Druid Knot lay in three pieces. Its intricate woven metal strands had been crushed and broken by the falling section of wall.

Liam was exhausted. His reserves were all but gone and his resolve had drained away. Kerri had shown herself to be more than what he had suspected. Perhaps he could do a bit more community service for the Preservers, as long as he was sent with Kerri Quinn.

As Liam caught his breath, Kerri tested the veil. She touched the broach attached to her blouse with one hand and then spread the fingers of her other hand out in front of her. There was a faint blue-green glow that stretched in a transparent wall to either side of her outstretched hand.

"I love the feel of the veil, its warmth and softness. I used to play within the veil itself when I was younger."

Liam ignored her reminisce. "What's next, Kerri?"

She closed her hand and the glow died away. "Just one before we head back to the fairy. We lost a knot when it was discovered. Its strength has been weakened because of where it is now. We think it might be in a museum in a village of Dublin."

"Wait, not another museum. I didn't agree to come along to go into another museum." *I should have killed her.*

"Scared of the guards?" Her smile was as broad as before, white teeth sparkling out from behind a muddy face.

"No, I just don't like those places."

"Bet I beat you." She wrapped her cloak around herself and set off running down the turf to the castle's curtain wall.

"I bet you will, too. You didn't tell me where the museum was in that village. I bet they have more than one." He still had time to kill her if she irritated him enough. Besides, the Treorai must want her dead for another reason than just losing a map. There had to be more to it. But he didn't know what that was.

Liam pulled up his hood and ran for the wall that surrounded the ancient castle. His long strides allowed him to catch up to Kerri quickly.

In a single leap they flew like shadows over the lichen-encrusted wall and were gone.

The grass it did tickle Sean's toes,
While his love licked the tip of his...nose.
His hand it did sneak,
Flipped her skirt for a peek,
And found she was Seamus, not Rose!

—Val Ford
First place, limerick contest

In my early teens I read The Sun Also Rises and immediately fell in love with Ernest Hemingway. I also knew at some point in time, that I, too, would travel and write about my adventures. It took me over forty years to do it, but better late than never.

REFLECTIONS OF A RETIRED BLACK WOMAN

by Gail Harris

When it comes to seeking insights, I like to paraphrase that saying about NFL Football: if you have an open mind, it can hit you on any given day.

In February 2006, I quit my job and moved to a small resort town in Colorado. Family and friends thought I'd had a nervous breakdown, but it made perfect sense to me. After a lifetime of working 80-plus hour weeks with very little time off, I decided to spend the rest of my life doing whatever I felt inspired or led to do. That's how I found myself standing in front of Saint Patrick's Cathedral in Dublin, Ireland scratching my head.

As a participant in a writing class, I'd been given the task of wandering around Dublin looking for inspiration for a short story, essay, or whatever. The assignment had to be completed in two and half hours. Most of my classmates were fiction writers while my background was in geopolitical topics. I didn't know how wandering around staring at people for a couple of hours was going to give me a nonfiction topic to write about, but I had nothing to lose but a little professional pride. On a whim I'd decided to check out the church. All I knew about Saint Patrick was that he had driven the snakes out of Ireland. I have a big snake phobia so that resonated very strongly with me.

I started walking around the outside of the church, still wondering what the heck I was doing. I didn't see many people around and wondered if it was even open. I noticed a plaque on the grounds and went over and looked at it. It said that was the spot it was believed Saint Patrick had baptized many Christian converts. I looked around to make sure no one was watching, touched the plaque, then rubbed my hand over my sinuses. Traditional medicine hadn't helped; who knows maybe "woo woo" would.

I decided to stop stalling and go on in. As I wandered around the church, guide book in hand, staring at plaques, two facts jumped out at me. At one point in his life, Saint Patrick had been a slave. He had been born in Britain to a well-off family and at the age of sixteen, he was kidnapped, taken to Ireland, and made a slave. The other surprise was that Jonathan Swift, who I knew only as the author of *Gulliver's Travels*, was a cleric who had been Dean of the Cathedral from 1713-1745.

The church started to fill up with tourists, so I found a quiet nook and pondered why those two things grabbed my attention. Slavery—there's a hot button. As an African American, I was particularly sensitive to that issue. It's a subject frequently ignored or glossed over in history books. In a February 3, 2003 National Geographic article, Howard Dodson stated "of the 6.5 million immigrants who survived the crossing of the Atlantic between 1492 and 1776, only 1 million were Europeans, 5.5 million were Africans." In spite of that fact, in books or movies depicting that era, black people are rarely shown or mentioned.

I think the reason for this is not necessarily malice but embarrassment that a nation founded on the principle of liberty and justice for all had to go through a bloody civil war in the nineteenth century, followed by a civil rights movement nearly a hundred years later, to make this a reality for a large segment of the population.

Learning that Saint Patrick was once a slave reminded me that slavery wasn't just an American issue but a worldwide issue. It still exists in the world today in various horrible forms. The press is filled with reports of children from Third World countries bought to western countries (including our own) and used as sex slaves. It is a horrible situation, and I believe we need to study the past, and learn from it so we don't repeat the abuses. If used correctly, international institutions like the United Nations can go a long way toward stamping out this abomination.

I found the fact that Saint Patrick returned to Ireland as a missionary after he had escaped and gained his freedom all the more remarkable. He apparently had forgiven the people who enslaved him. He went from being part of the lowest segment of Irish society to being that nation's patron Saint; a true testament to the power of one and the power of forgiveness.

There was a lot of information about Jonathan Swift at the cathedral but the thing that impressed me the most was a quote from his book "Thoughts on Various Subjects": "We have just enough religion to make us hate, but not enough to make us love one another." Swift wrote that in 1728 and it still applies several centuries later.

Throughout history there have been a lot of atrocities committed in the name of religion. I find it ironic. I'm no expert, but I've noticed a lot of commonality among the world's major religions. I've spent some time in the Middle East and was surprised to learn that a lot of figures in the Christian religion are also revered in Islam.

Wouldn't it be wonderful if we spent more time finding out what we had in common than talking about differences? Wouldn't it be great if someone from a conservative background in the Middle East saw a western woman walking down the street with her head uncovered and knew she was dressed that way not because she was a "Hoochie Mama" but because she was just reflecting the way woman of her culture dressed? Wouldn't it be great if I never again assumed that a woman dressed in a veil with only her eyes showing was a persecuted minority? Turned out a woman who approached me at a party in the Middle East, dressed just so, was a well-known architect. Showed how much I knew about the culture. I figured she'd just escaped from a harem.

Hatred and prejudice has its basis in fear and ignorance.

I'm reminded of the end of one of my favorite movies, "The Day the Earth Stood Still". Michael Rennie played an alien ambassador who had been sent to earth. Of course we earthlings tried to lock him up and kill him. Presumably our scientists wanted to dissect him or something. He escaped and at the end before he took off in his space ship, he spoke before a delegation of world scientists. Basically, he told them that people from space have been watching us for centuries and don't like what they see. We are mean, petty and warlike. Now that we were beginning to travel in space, we have the potential to interact with advanced life elsewhere. He was sent to tell us we'd better get our act together or else earth would cease to exist.

I'm not expecting a visitor from outer space, but I do know that if we don't learn how to get along, we have weapons that could destroy most of known civilization. We need to get along not just because it's the right thing to do, but because it's necessary for our survival as a species.

At St. Patrick's, I looked at my watch and saw I had better be heading back to rendezvous with my class and teachers. My views are my own, I'm just your average aging Baby Boomer, but as I ambled along, I realized that inspiration can come on any given day and in surprising environments.

The inspiration for this piece was the ambiance of Ireland, land of faeries, leprechauns, banshees, and so on. I took John Saul's "What If?" exercise, applied it to guardian angels, and this is how it turned out.

Angel Aware

by Ardith Ashton

Lydia thought she saw something from the corner of her eye—a white flash, as if something, or someone, were moving very quickly. Trying to stay out of view? Her nerve endings told her someone was watching her, the hairs standing out on the back of her neck. She wasn't familiar with this city after all, and she was trying to be super cautious, aware of her surroundings, as they taught her in self-defense class.

She'd come to Dublin as a tourist with a group, and had a free afternoon enjoying a bit of shopping and a walkabout.

She passed the flower stall on a corner of Grafton Street, and the scent of lilies followed her down the block. Delightful. One of the restaurants was serving fish today, she could smell. The chocolatier had large fans blowing the smell of his wares into the street to tempt passersby. Same with the baker, as Lydia could detect the aroma of baking bread on the morning breeze.

What a morning, she thought. The air was magic. The sun was shining, and its warmth was comforting. She drew a lungful of the intoxicating air and felt on top of the world. She wanted to skip and sing like a seven-year-old, and just glory in being, in spite of the slight sense of unease which had already begun to fade. Her thoughts tumbled about each other like bubbles in a glass of soda, hanging on the edges and making her dizzy with their intensity. Or was it just breathing the air?

The crowd thinned the farther she got from Grafton Street, and soon she noticed there was no one on the streets, and thought that was odd. There was no accounting for the absence of people, unless she'd come further than she thought.

She came to the corner, looked both ways and stepped off the curb, still wondering if what she'd felt earlier was significant in any way.

Suddenly, a car came screeching around the corner, and she didn't have time to jump out of the way. She would have been struck, but at the last split-second, someone grabbed her arm and pulled her to safety. They both fell to the side-walk in an untidy heap of limbs and Lydia's packages. The man was dressed in a white suit and was a very good look-ing individual. There was a certain radiance about him—almost an incandescence.

Lydia's pulse was reacting to the jolt of adrenaline, and it was a few moments before she felt as if her legs would support her, so she pulled herself to a sitting position and looked more closely at her rescuer. He had white hair and the greenest eyes she'd ever seen. His eyes crinkled at the corners when he smiled at her.

"I'm sure lucky you were there," she gasped. "Thank you so much!"

"Welcome." His voice was deep and resonant.

"I'm Lydia Martin," she said, offering her hand which he took carefully. His touch was so light, Lydia wasn't sure she could feel it.

"I'm Michael," he said after just a short hesitation.

"Where did you come from?" she inquired. "I didn't see anybody else on the street."

"I was there," he said, gesturing vaguely over his shoul-der.

Her pulse normal enough to allow her to rise, Lydia got to her feet. Michael helped her collect her various posses-sions.

"Well, thanks again. Maybe I'll see you around," Lydia said, hoping he'd ask her to have tea with him. She wanted to get better acquainted with him, but the invitation was not forthcoming, and she walked away.

Her tourist group was going to Killarney and doing a

tour of the Ring of Kerry that would take a few days, but Lydia decided she didn't want to spend time on the bus among those people, moving all her luggage each time they stayed in a different hotel. She decided she'd stay in Dublin for a few days more. She could rejoin the group later when they returned, then continue their tour.

Back at her hotel, she was reading someone's essay on angels in a magazine she'd pick up. The words seemed to look as if they were in boldface type. *Guardian Angels.* Hmmm. Was her subconscious trying to tell her something? When she looked a second time, the words were all the same, none in boldface.

Lydia did not have a religious background, having been raised by a couple of agnostics, so had never really thought much about angels of any kind, guardian or otherwise.

Her mind went back to the episode with Michael. That name was too... too... what? Corny? Clichéd? Both?

She had seen *no one else* on the street or sidewalk at all before that car came around the corner. She didn't recall seeing any doorways from which he could have materialized... *Materialized.* That was it! He'd come out of nowhere, suddenly, like a flash. He was wearing a white suit. Was that the flash of white she'd seen moments before the incident? She tried to remember, to reconstruct the time leading up to the near-tragedy. What was it she had experienced? She'd had the overpowering sense of well-being, then she'd seen something. What?

Just a flash of white, and felt the hairs on the back of her neck react to... what? She wasn't usually into psychic or supernatural things. In fact, she'd *never* experienced anything remotely like this before.

She was probably imagining some "woo-woo" Twilight Zone happening, and she shook herself mentally to rid herself of the idea. But as the time passed, she kept coming back to the incident, searching for an explanation. She found herself thinking about the man who had pulled her out of harm's way. Who was he, really? Where did he come from, and would she ever see him again? She hoped so. In his presence, she felt…safe. Safe and loved. There was nothing in her world to make her feel unsafe, but she liked the feeling she'd had when Michael was there.

She took to looking or him every time she went out, and sometimes she thought she'd caught a glimpse of him in a crowd, or down the block, but when she took a better look, or followed him down the street, it always turned out to be someone else.

Frustrated, she began to actively search for him. She went into places that were less than genteel, pubs where alcohol-soaked denizens lurked. To Lydia, these places were frightening, but she was driven by an obsession to find Michael.

One afternoon late, she was waylaid in the street near one of those sleazy pubs. She'd been making her way down the dirty sidewalk, looking for the familiar white suit, when someone gripped her arm.

"Come, girlie, let's go into the alley," said a rough voice.

Mentally cursing her inattention to locale, thus violating the first rule of self-defense, Lydia struggled and tried to do what the self-defense instructor had trained her to do, but the attacker already had hold of her. She twisted, trying to get an elbow into his face, but he was too tall. She tried to stomp on his instep, but he lifted her off her feet and pulled her into a doorway in the next building and pushed her into a dirty room. She opened her mouth to scream and yell, but he hit her so hard her brain buzzed.

"If you don't be quiet, I'll hit you again," he said in a low voice.

He pulled at her clothes and was fumbling with his own trousers when he was violently knocked to one side. He slid down the wall, eyes shut, and settled on the floor. Hands drew Lydia up, pressed her against a strong chest, covered by a white suit. Tears flowed down her cheeks, and she leaned into Michael's strength.

"Shhh." His hands rubbed her back, comforting her. "Easy, now. It's all right."

"I was looking for you," Lydia sobbed. "I-I couldn't find you."

He held her until she stopped crying, which was a while. The lump of flesh on the floor in the corner gave a groan, which signaled his coming to.

"I think I'd better get you home," Michael said.

Without asking her address, he walked Lydia to her hotel.

"Will you come in?" she invited.

He hesitated briefly. "For just a moment," he answered. "Then I must go."

Her cheek where she'd been struck was bruised and swelling, so she put ice on it when she got to her room. Michael sat in the living room, fidgeting uncomfortably.

"Michael, thank you again for helping me."

Lydia wondered just how it was that he was always so conveniently near when she needed help, but she wouldn't allow her mind to accept the impossible. Guardian angels, indeed! And why was he so nervous about being in the apartment of a grateful woman whom he'd just saved from a fate worse than death?

"I will go now, if you're all right," he said, and rose effortlessly. Lydia was not an expert in geriatrics, but it seemed that someone Michael's apparent age should have stiff knees, or something that would make his joints creak, but Michael moved like a kid. Everything about him said "youth" except for the way he looked.

"Oh. Well, you're my guardian angel, Michael, and I—"

He blanched, then looked around him, as if searching for something. Or somebody. His unexpected reaction to her words startled her.

"Lydia, I shall leave you now," he said, opening the door and stepping out.

"I was going to make coffee," she said to his retreating back.

What was going on? He seemed so furtive and uncomfortable. Lydia puzzled over this for a while. He'd reacted when she said "guardian angel."

Thee it was again. Guardian Angel. Lydia had never believed in such things, but... was it possible?

She thought she'd put her idea to the test. She'd have to be careful, however. She didn't want to do herself any harm, but she needed to see if Michael would save her once again.

A couple of days went by as she planned her stunt. It had to look authentic, but present no real danger to her. That would be difficult, finding such a situation. Meanwhile, she walked the streets around her hotel, enjoying the ambience of the town. Dublin was a thriving city. It was busy and crowded, and Lydia found it delightful. On one of her walks, she came upon two old ladies doing a slow two-step with their canes.

"I think it's time for tea," one of them quavered.

"Right you are, and it's my turn to buy," said her companion, putting out a hand to steady herself against the side of the building.

Lydia thought the older lady was going to fall, so she put out her hand, catching the woman's elbow as she went down. She pulled the old lady up, then stood a moment as the woman caught her breath.

"Thank you, dearie," the woman said with a smile that made Lydia feel much like a guardian angel herself.

She worked on her plan to see if Michael would save her. She could just step off another curb in front of an approaching vehicle, but there was the possibility she was imagining this whole angel thing, and she might really be hurt or killed. She didn't want that. The idea of taking a blade and slitting her wrists also crossed her mind, but the thought of lying bleeding, hoping the maid would come in to do her room and find her wasn't practical. If the maid were late that day, Lydia would exsanguinate. She had to think of something that would reveal the truth about Michael.

The day before the touring group was due to return to Dublin and Lydia would have to rejoin them, she had an opportunity to test her idea. She knew the maid would soon be there to turn down the bed and would probably find her in time, so she simply went to her medicine bag and took out her sleeping pills.

"Okay, Michael," she said to her empty room. "I'm going to take these pills. All of them."

No answer.

"I mean it, Michael. I really do."

Silence.

She got a glass of water and began taking the pills, one by one.

She'd taken four, probably not yet a lethal dose, and turned around to see Michael sitting on the couch.

"Is this really what you want to do?" he asked. "If it is, I won't stop you."

"I had to find out if you really existed," Lydia said.

"Aren't you going to purge your system?" he asked.

After Lydia got rid of the pills, she went back to the living room area.

"You aren't supposed to know about me," he scolded.

"I don't believe in you," Lydia murmured. "At least I didn't until now."

"That makes it even worse," he said. "You humans *can't* know about us; we work in secret."

"Like the CIA," Lydia whispered.

Michael sighed.

"Rest now. You'll be okay."

"Stay with me?" Lydia pleaded.

"I can't. It's against the rules."

"Screw the rules. I need you."

"I'll stay until you fall asleep."

When Lydia awoke the next morning, he was gone. Her group would be here today and she'd have to move.

She finally realized that Michael had always been there, taking care of her, keeping her from harm.

"Michael, I know you're there," she said aloud. "I know you watch over me."

There was no answer, but she hadn't expected one.

"I'm sure you've been there all my life, and I want to thank you."

Her voice echoed in the silence.

"I know," she said impishly. "I can take up mountain climbing and bungee jumping and sky diving!"

She thought she heard an exasperated sigh and a quiet "You brat!"

But it could have been her imagination.

I wrote this ballad after following around Liz Engstrom Cratty's husband, Al Cratty (not to be confused just yet with Old Al Crotty)□while he searched the streets and byways of Kilkenny, Ireland, for visual evidence of the fate of his like-named ancestor. Al knew coming over from the wilds of Oregon that the Crotty's were infamous in certain parts of Ireland, and that one of them—a Lord Mayor of the town, no less—had been hanged some centuries back for an unnamed crime. Al's intent was to discover the truth about this unfortunate and about Crottys in general.

The first thing he was told by the locals, if I recall correctly, on asking about Crottys, was that they were well known and generally hanged at the first opportunity. That didn't seem particularly auspicious, but Al was sure this was a generalization. He did, however, quit giving out his last name. The search continued. There were lots of Crottys in the phone books, but no museum or National Trust site that might commemorate Old Al. Eventually, Young Al was able to find the spot on which his ancestor, Old Al, was executed back in the 1600s. Or somewhere back in the past, anyway. Before electricity, I'm certain. Anyway, the spot was occupied currently by a toy store or an ice cream parlor or maybe a parking meter. There was no plaque. No record of the event could be found.

But Al—Al Cratty, not Crotty—was told by someone, maybe the bus driver, that his ancestor was hung either for thievery or buggery. Since there was no way of determining which without extensive research, I felt free to exercise artistic license and choose which offense I wanted to use for purposes of this writing. Al said he didn't care. But he was pretty definite about not using his name in the writing. I have honored his wishes.

And so, without further blather,

THE HANGING OF OLD AL CROTTY
(A BALLAD)
by Terry Brooks

'Tis midday in Kilkenny with the sun a'shining down.
And the women and the children have gathered all in
town.
Yes, the weepin' and the wailin' can be heard a mile away.
They're hanging Old Al Crotty from the castle walls today.

T'was not his fault his eyesight failed when first he saw the
lass.
Colleen was sweet, and she did bleat with a special kind of
sass.
But townfolk are judgmental and fixed upon their way.
They're hanging old Al Crotty from the castle walls today.

T'was a small offense committed. But a single sheep
involved.
Still, the act was done quite public, and the crime was
quickly solved.
T'was not the sheep that testified but the shepherd she'd
betrayed.
They're hanging Old Al Crotty from the castle walls today.

T'was not a crime that merited the punishment it found.
But the Lord Mayor's fickle public would not suffer him a
clown.
So was his fate decided by the vagaries of his day.
They're hanging Old Al Crotty from the castle walls today.

T'will be a sight quite terrible when from the wall he
drops.
His neck will snap, his tongue extend, his joints and

sockets pop.
Drawn and quartered, this poor old soul, and then his
 flesh they'll flay.
They're hanging Old Al Crotty from the castle walls today.

They'll use a hammer on his toes; they'll smash them one
 by one.
And then they'll light a fire 'neath his gnarly old man's
 bum.
And when the fire's consumed him, they'll haul his bones
 away.
They're hanging Old Al Crotty from the castle walls today.

Somewhere the sun is shining, and children are at play.
Somewhere right-thinking men and women know that it's
 okay
To love a sheep or e'en a goat and frolic in the hay.
And not be judged a bugger and go Al Crotty's way.

My inspiration for this story came from a trip I made to an antique store in Adare, on a wet and windy day in May, 2006. I found a tiny tea set, and was intrigued by the name: Bachelor Tea Set. As we left the shop and strolled back to Adare Manor, we walked along the main street, admiring the beautiful, tidy cottages that lined the street. We began to walk past one which was in a state of abandonment. The front lawn was waist deep in tall grass, weeds, and dandelions. The cottage was dark and hadn't been lived in for some time, by the looks of the place. I noticed many dandelion seeds, all waiting to be wished upon. I connected the tea set and abandoned cottage, and imagined a sad little old man, alone, drinking his tea, dying with no family or heirs, and his things sent off to the antique store for disposition. I saw the dandelions and thought how sad that all the wishes and dreams of the owner of the cottage hadn't come true, but the dreams and wishes were still there, just waiting for someone to come along and claim them.

A Promise to Return

by Stacy Allen

"It's nearly one and I am starving. Can't this wait?" Jonathan said, planting his feet firmly against the sidewalk in Adare, Ireland. They stood on the outside of a small, bright yellow door with a sign that read "Antiques".

"Yes, Jonathan, it can. As a matter of fact, it can wait forever," Faith said, yanking the door open and letting it close behind her, rattling and ringing as a tiny bell chimed out against the doorknob.

"*Jesus,*" he whispered, shrugging his shoulders as he watched her disappear into the little shop, then followed.

He walked to the back room which was filled to overflowing with old books and photos. He saw traces of her bright orange scarf flitting amongst the stacks of oddments which were wedged and tucked everywhere in the room.

It was quiet in the shop except the faint strains of orchestral music lilting from an open doorway in the back. He walked toward the orange vision that was darting in and out of sight. He found Faith standing in front a bookshelf, studying a row of old apothecary bottles, some with labels barely legible.

"Are you looking for a present, then? Is this your young gentleman?" A woman appeared from behind the bookcase and glanced at Jonathan who stood rigid, his hands in his wool jacket pockets.

"We're looking for a gift for Jonathan's mother." Faith answered, which brought a smile to the older woman.

"Does she collect antiques?" the woman said as she dusted and arranged items on a long wooden table, its surface marred with decades of use.

"Well, Jonathan's fortieth birthday was a few weeks ago, and this trip was her gift. She spent some time here many years ago. A summer, I think. She collects silver tea sets, and that one is so unique. I think it would be a nice present to take back to her. Different from anything she has. Can you tell me the history of it?"

"Oh yes, the tea set. Well, love, Mister O'Halloran, he lived here his whole life. He was a bit of a recluse," the woman offered, moving a stack of old magazines and newspapers and placing them in a neat stack on the corner of the table. "Would you like to see it again?" the woman asked.

"I'd love to," Faith answered, reaching for Jonathan, squeezing his forearm in her excitement.

The woman walked to shelf and reached, standing on tip-toes, carefully removing the tiny silver tea set, one piece at a time, setting it on a bright red cashmere scarf she had draped across the dark wooden table top. It gleamed in the light. Faith's fingers delicately stroked the handle.

"Go on then, dear. You can touch it," the woman urged her. Faith smiled and gently lifted the tiny tea pot. It was only about four inches tall, she estimated. It would hold just a cup. The cream and sugar were tiny also, maybe two inches tall. Tiny and delicate, but it all looked authentic, not like a toy.

Faith imagined the tea set full of steaming hot liquid, next to a lonely old bachelor, sitting in a rocking chair on his covered porch. Perhaps he was even smoking a pipe, a heavy Irish rain pouring down around him. She imagined a woolen shawl covering his slender legs.

"Faith," Jonathan finally spoke. She turned and met his gaze, then set the pot back down on the red shawl. They walked to the front of the store to speak privately.

Her face softened "Look, Jonathan, if you want to go eat first, let's do that. We can always come back after lunch," Faith said, walking toward the front door. The woman came up front, interrupting their discussion.

"We've decided to get some lunch, and then come back in a little while," Jonathan spoke quickly to countermand the situation, before being drawn into an afternoon of hot tea and long-winded stories of Ireland. He'd heard enough of those from his mother. He wouldn't even be in Adare if it hadn't been for his mother's insistence. She was obsessed with Ireland.

"We should really go, we're hungry and exhausted from walking much of the morning," Faith smiled down at the tiny lady on the other side of the wooden table

"You'll be back then?"

Faith smiled and nodded. "What time do you close?" she asked. *A promise to return.*

"Oh I live in the back, I'm always here. I lock the doors at six, but if you make your decision tonight, just give me a call and drop by, and I'll let you in," the woman answered, handing her a business card from a pocket in her apron.

"We'll just run get some lunch and perhaps a nap, then we'll come back this afternoon, or this evening," Faith promised.

She and Jonathan made their way to the front door and escaped into the mid-day gloom of Adare, a light sprinkle tickling their faces and dampening their hair.

"Will you please slow down?" Faith struggled to match Jonathan's strides. He slowed his pace slightly as she came up alongside, but then resumed his brisk steps. When Jonathan was hungry, nothing got in his way.

She suppressed the urge to slap him. She loved him madly, but sometimes he was an inconsiderate ass. *He knows I can't keep up with his long damn legs.*

It wasn't like she was asking for the moon . . . just basic consideration. She wasn't even asking for a ring. She hadn't brought up marriage in months, though thoughts of marrying Jonathan often swelled and crested through her.

Faith's short legs stretched out as far as possible, and her calves felt tight and angry. Her muscles were sore from all this harsh, fast clomping about in Ireland. She had run out of band aids doctoring the red blisters she had managed to get tromping about old ruins and modern monuments. It seemed as though Jonathan rushed her from one thing to another, without allowing her to slow down and appreciate what was in front of them.

"I can't help it, Faith, I'm starving," he said, slowing slightly to allow her to catch up again. He leaned down and ran his hands through a loose tendril that floated around her delicate face and they stopped momentarily on the sidewalk in front of a row of shops. A butcher, a dry cleaner, and a jewelry store.

She stopped, allowing the moment time to fully mature. Leaning into his cupped palm, she closed her eyes and breathed in. The scent of lilacs and recent rain saturated the air around them, and Faith opened her eyes.

They had been together, on and off, for nearly eight years, and they had taken many trips together, but this time the space between them felt different.

The moment passed. Jonathan turned and continued walking and she took in the sight of him for a split second before continuing to follow him. He was tall, strong, firmly built. He was an architectural engineer and a brilliant man. He was loving most of the time, considerate often, and he loved slapstick comedy and thriller movies. But would all that a good husband make?

She felt sure he never spent time obsessing about things like marriage and children and love and relationships.

She wouldn't mention marriage again. Too many times

she had broached the subject and too many times they had come to a stalemate. She had come to a decision and made a silent pronunciation that this trip together would likely be their last if this issue did not resolve soon. She'd even talked to Carolyn, Jonathan's mother, about her frustration. If he wanted to propose, it had to be his decision, made as a result of his love for her. But not because Faith had nagged him to finally quit stalling.

They rounded the corner, his steps in front of hers and his pace quickening again, as if they were rushing to make a train.

They walked into the Dunraven Arms pub, leaving the cold, March rain outside for the warmth inside. The room felt comforting after walking hours in the biting Irish rain.

"Irish stew, please. And a pint," he said to the waitress who had come to their table. He handed her back both menus, and Faith took one of them back.

"I actually need another minute to decide, thanks," she said. "But I'll take a half pint in the meantime," she said, opening the well-worn, plastic-covered menu.

Jonathan looked at Faith, impatient for her to pick something out from the limited list in front of her. "We've been here so many times in the past week, I assumed you would get the roast chicken. That's all you ever order," he said.

"Well, today I want something different," she snapped. "On second thought, I'm not hungry. You eat, and go take a nap. You'll be easier to be around," Faith said, standing and gathering her purse, wrapping her orange scarf loosely around her neck.

She didn't wait for a response before turning and heading out into the wet April afternoon.

She headed back to the antique shop, reaching for the large brass knob on the heavily-lacquered door.

Faith was determined to leave the shop with the tea set in hand.

"I am back. Wrap it up," she said to the shop keeper, no further discussion necessary. *She* would buy it for Jonathan's mother, whom she adored.

"Very well then, dear. And I've got the original box it came in as well. Mr. O'Halloran kept it all these years," the woman said, going in the back and returning with a box that had yellowed over time. She opened it up, placing the tea set inside the velvet box with insets for the pieces. "There's a card underneath, if you care to keep that as well," she said casually as she put the lid on the box and placed it in a paper bag with handles before handing it to Faith. "Would you like some tea, then, dear? I'd love a break, and I'd love the company," the woman said.

"I'd love some tea," Faith responded. She needed to give Jonathan time to eat and sleep before she returned to the room.

She followed Mrs. O'Malley to the back room, where a small fire was burning, and they sat on a well-worn loveseat, sipping tea and chatting about nothing in particular, but enjoying one another's company. A few times the door jingled and Mrs. O'Malley helped a customer or two, and Faith drank the tea and felt peaceful in front of the warmth of the fire.

"Thank you so much," Faith said, turning down a third cup of tea. It was nearly two and the caffeine would keep her up if she had a third cup.

She took the bag, walking slowly back toward Adare Manor, admiring the cottages that lined the main street that headed out of town. One after another, cottages lined up, flowers neatly arranged, with the lawns well manicured. The little doors and windows looked inviting and friendly, and Faith felt like she was walking in a fairy tale. Nearing the end of the row of cottages, Faith stopped in her tracks when she found herself in front of a cottage that looked abandoned. Nestled between two neat-as-a-pin homes, she was surprised to see this home in such a state of neglect.

Weeds, dandelions, and grass were nearly waist deep and there were no flowers blooming anywhere. A sea of dandelion had gone to seed, and Faith remembered making wishes on them as a young girl. This yard had at least fifty of them, all waiting to be used for wish-making.

Faith was overwhelmed by a sense of sadness when she

saw the cottage, and imagined that the owner must have left, giving up on his or her hopes and dreams, thinking they would never come true. Yet to Faith, here they all were, just waiting for someone to come along and claim them.

What can it hurt? She set the bag from the antique store down before reaching across the small wooden gate and snapping off a dandelion. She closed her eyes and made her wish, opening them again and blowing as hard as she could to remove all the seeds from the stem. They floated into the yard, and Faith smiled. It was the same wish she had made year after year. It probably wouldn't come true, but she was named Faith for some reason. Perhaps just this once it would. She wouldn't give up dreaming. She picked up the bag and continued on through the large gate of Adare and through the grounds to the manor house.

She found Jonathan awake from his nap and preparing to take a hot bath. They didn't speak, Faith preoccupied with removing the tea set from the bag, and Jonathan pretending there was nothing wrong. He reached for his book and disappeared into the bathroom.

When she heard him running the water, Faith reached for the phone and her calling card, dialing while she had the rare privacy.

Jonathan's mother answered on the first ring, though Faith could hear her making gardening noises. Carolyn gardened daily. Even in the winter, she would spread out a tarp on the dining table and fuss with pots and plants, even if just to water and trim them. As long as she had her hands on earth and growing things, she was happy.

"We're having a great time here, Carolyn," Faith said, stretching across the bed on her belly and resting on her bent elbows.

"What's wrong? Is Jonathan being a jerk?" Carolyn asked.

"No, not a jerk, exactly," Faith replied, feeling strange. Talking to a woman who calls her own son a jerk was almost amusing. At least Carolyn knew her own son.

"But nothing's been said, obviously. You've been there nearly two weeks," Carolyn sounded exasperated. She loved her son, but he was thick-headed when it came to the subject of marriage.

"Well, Carolyn, I can't make him *want* to marry me. He either does or he doesn't. I can't force the issue. I won't bring it up. I won't." Before the trip, Faith had declared to Carolyn that after eight years together, if Jonathan didn't make some proclamation of lifelong love and commitment, she was moving on

"You leave Ireland tomorrow?" Carolyn asked, but it was more of a statement. "Faith, I don't know what to tell you. I think you two are perfect for one another. And I understand your need to want to be married and start a family. But my son is obstinate, bless him. Obstinate and bull-headed."

"I know," Faith whispered, dropping her elbows and rolling on her back, staring at the ceiling of their hotel suite.

She heard Jonathan running more hot water in the tub. She had a few more minutes of privacy at least.

"Listen, Faith. You must resolve this. I left Adare, and I have always regretted that decision. I can't turn back time, but I can tell you that if you leave Adare and you and Jonathan haven't decided to stay together, then you will surely part," she said.

"Well I can't make him do anything. Believe me, I have mentioned marriage, many times. But I won't give him an ultimatum. I shouldn't have to. Either he loves me or he doesn't."

"Have him call me when he is out of his bath," Carolyn said.

"I will. Love you," Faith said, and hung up. She got off the bed, and went to the table where the tea set was wrapped up in tissue paper and tiny bubble wrap. Carefully she unwrapped it and set each piece on the table.

Jonathan emerged, wrapped in a thick robe, a bath towel around his shoulders to catch the drips from his wet brown hair which curled slightly around his neck and shoulders.

He rubbed at his ears with the towel, and Faith smiled, her heart melting at the sight of him all wet and mussed.

"I called your mother and caught up. She wants you to

call her," she said, crossing the room and kissing him intently, but with closed lips.

"I hope you left some hot water for me," she teased, as she entered the bathroom. "Don't forget to call your mother," she said, and gently closed the door.

Jonathan dried and dressed before reaching for the calling card, which was perched by the telephone. He dialed his mother's number with reluctance.

"Hey Mom," he said, punching up the pillows behind him and relaxing back on the headboard.

"Jonathan, what the hell are you doing?" she started, shocking him. He could hear the strain in her voice.

"Have you been crying?" he asked. "Are you crying?" he asked again.

"Listen to what I have to say," she said.

"What is the matter?"

"Do you want to know why I sent you to Ireland?" she asked.

"Of course I know, you spent time here when you were younger and you loved it and you never had a chance to return. And you wanted me to see its beauty. And you wanted Faith and I to have a vacation, because we hadn't taken one in so long."

"Yes, all of those reasons are true. But they aren't the only ones. You know that I was in Adare the summer after I graduated from college. You know that I spent four months there visiting a distant aunt."

Jonathan, impatient, had heard this before. "Yeah, I know—"

"Don't interrupt me. I'm not finished."

The line was quiet for a moment before she continued. "I lived in Adare for the summer, and I met a young man who helped my aunt with her lawn work. He was saving money to go to school, and in the afternoon, when my aunt napped, we would sit and talk on the porch sometimes when he took his breaks. I won't go into the details, but through the summer we fell in love. We began to see one another every day, and every night. When the summer was coming to a close, I asked him if I should stay. He said no, he was going away to school, and I had to go home. In a year or two we might be able to be together again. I promised to return to him, if he would ask me to come. Only he never asked, and I never insisted." Her voice faltered and Jonathan could hear her crying slightly.

"After that August, he went off to Trinity College and I came home. We never saw each other again."

"Why not?"

"It doesn't matter why not, Jonathan. We just didn't. We could sit here all day and theorize as to why it didn't happen. But that doesn't matter. What does matter is we had an opportunity to be together forever and we didn't follow through. He didn't follow through. I didn't follow through. Once I got home, I had other issues to attend to. I had to get on with my life, though I yearned for him and missed him every day. I couldn't find a way to speak up then. But I can now. If you are foolish enough to let Faith slip through your fingers, then you aren't the man I raised you to be. I can't seem to make you understand that, and neither can she. This is your last chance with her, don't you realize that?"

"Faith and I are fine, Mom," he started.

"You are not fine, Jonathan. Faith wants to get married and have children and you just ignore that fact. You think every day you go through the motions, and every day you are happy. You don't see that at the end of all those days, you will be left alone and sit there wondering what happened and why Faith left. There is more to life than just this day, Jonathan. There are days after today, and days after that. There are many, many days and all strung together, they make a life. Your life. Don't waste the future because you can't seem to get beyond right now."

"I love Faith, Mom, I do. I just don't know why we have to be married for her to know that."

"Because you'll be saying to her finally, once and for all, you love her enough to risk your whole lifetime. You love her enough to say to the world that you don't care what tomorrow has in store, because you have her by your side. You love her enough that nothing will stand in the way of you two being together forever. Right now, either one of you can walk away with no consequences except broken hearts. When you get married, you say *I'm in it for the long haul. I can do this.* You don't hedge your bets and keep one foot on the doorstep and one on the porch. You don't always leave yourself room to sneak out the back. That means something. That tells her you are hers, no matter what. And that she is yours no matter what. You have a chance to make the right choice. Don't waste it."

"Faith knows I love her."

"Yes, Jonathan, you're right. Faith knows you love her. But Faith doesn't believe that you love her enough. That is the difference."

"I'll think about it, Mom. I will. I am going to go now. I love you."

He hung up the phone, staring at it for a few minutes. He could hear Faith singing softly, the water splashing about her, and he smiled. She still acted like a kid when she was in a bubble bath. He loved that about her.

He noticed the tea set and walked to it, picking up the pieces for the first time. It *was* beautiful. Turning it over, he noticed the label from the antique shop that read *Bachelor Tea Set* and the price. He tugged gently at the sticker, taking care to remove it in one piece, sticking it on a corner of the tissue paper where Faith could have it for her scrapbook. She was sentimental and silly and loved mementos.

He rubbed the bottom with his thumb to remove the small amount of adhesive residue. He could see an engraving, and he walked to the lamp by the bed, reaching for his reading glasses to see it clearer. He read it carefully, his eyes blinking and tearing up slightly. The date was late August, 41 years prior. This was the end of March and he had just celebrated his fortieth birthday. It wasn't possible, was it?

He read the inscription again and shook his head slightly before putting the tiny tea pot back on the desk next to the equally small creamer and sugar bowl. He saw the gift card sticking out from under a corner of the velvet and he reached for it. The ink was faded, but he could make out the message, blinking his eyes a few times before replacing it inside the box under the velvet.

"Hey honey, I am going out for a walk, but I'll be back by six or so," he yelled through the door.

"Okay, see you in a bit," she replied, then continued her singing until she had finished the last verse of Danny Boy. It always made her cry. The poor woman waited forever for Danny to return to her, and she was cold in her grave but still hung on to the belief that Danny Boy would return to her and say he loved her at her gravestone. The Irish sure can write a tragic song, she thought, letting the bubbly water down the drain and standing to rinse off under a hot shower.

She was dressed and ready for dinner, tapping her fingers against her thighs. Where did he go? She pulled her jeans legs down over her boots. He must be starving, she thought, looking at the clock. It was nearly seven, and he said he would be back by six. Adare was a tiny village. What trouble could he have possibly found out on the streets of Adare?

When she heard the doorknob turn, she leaped to her feet as he came through the door.

"Sorry, I was just wandering and I totally lost track of time," he said, putting his arms around her for a hug as she crossed the room to him.

"I was beginning to think you had left me," she said, smiling and burying her head into his shoulder. "What did you do this afternoon? Where have you been?"

"I was walking around the grounds. I walked into town. I was thinking and walking and beating myself up. I'm an idiot. And I am a slow-learner. But I can get something, given enough time. I don't want to lose you. I don't want to end up like my father."

"Your father? I've never heard you mention your father," she said quietly.

"That's because I never knew anything about him. I was always told he was dead. Which he is."

"I don't understand," was her reply, and she leaned up and kissed the end of his chin.

He felt a tug at his heart. "Let's go eat, then. Can you grab my brush from the bathroom? I've been walking in the mist and wind, and I forgot my umbrella," he said.

She went into the bathroom, getting his brush from their travel bag and returning to find him sitting on the end of the bed, his coat off.

He took the brush from her outstretched hand and began to peer into the mirror over the desk as he slowly brushed his hair into place. "I stopped by the front desk and they said they have a packing box we can use to protect the tea set. I think we ought to wrap it well, though, and we should maybe wash it. I took the sticker off the bottom, but we should use some hot soapy water on it, to remove the fingerprints and tape residue. We can drop it off on our way to the dining room and they'll wrap it for us, but let's wash it first, inside and out." He kept brushing, moving the hairs back and forth, not appearing to accomplish much.

Faith, surprised that he was interested, picked up the tea set in both hands, cupping the pieces gently. She took them in to the bathroom and set them in the sink, starting the hot water and reaching for shampoo, the only liquid soap she had.

He quit brushing and tip-toed to the bathroom door and watched her. She washed and rinsed the creamer and sugar, and he entered, taking the dripping pieces from her and drying them on a linen hand towel. He was waiting, drying slowly, trying to prolong the process, when he saw her lift the lid of the tea pot and prepare to wash it. She gasped.

"Jonathan, look!" She was unable to get her hand inside the tiny pot, so she tipped it up and poured the contents into her right palm. "Look what I found!"

He smiled. "I know, I put it there," he said casually, though his heart was beating heavily in his chest. "When you were getting my hairbrush."

"Jonathan, really?" she was in shock. An engagement ring had slid into her wet palm, and he took it from her, shaking it slightly to remove the drips. She put down the tea pot and he slid it on her left finger without saying a word.

"This was his tea set. My mother gave it to him when she was here for that summer. I am his son. Look at the engraving on the bottom," he said, reaching for the pot and turning it over for her.

To S from C

25 Aug 65

"Come with me," he said, leading her back into the bedroom. He opened the box and lifted the velvet liner, removing the yellowed gift card and handing it to her. "I found this while you were singing in the tub," he said.

"To Sean, with love from Carolyn. I promise to return."

There once was a tailor named Glass
Who was a big pain in the ass
He stitched and he sewed
And passed a loud load
And from then on they called him Sir Gas!

—Bonnie Christoffersen and Aimée Carter

I arrived a day early for the writers' challenge, and found myself in the heart of Dublin on a glorious spring day, with the freedom to wander. I boarded a double-decker tour bus and rode around the city in the open air, viewing Ireland's capital from a bird's height. On the tour I learned the Viking's name for the city of two convergent rivers: 'Black Pool', or Dubh Lin, in Gaelic. I immediately decided that I would like to use this as the title for my story. Later, when I spotted an errant red balloon forlornly drifting in the dark water of the River Liffey, I had a vivid symbol around which my story developed.

Black Pool

by Carolyn Buchanan

The overcast sky threatened rain, but that was nothing new in Dublin. Since it wasn't actually raining yet, Allison pulled her dove gray Henley around her with bruised hands and turned from the sliding doors of the Westbury Hotel toward Grafton Street. She shivered in her coat, but it wasn't just the chill of the early spring morning, or the leaden skies that settled their weight on her thin shoulders.

"You need help, Allison," he had shouted, "serious, professional help."

At the corner of Grafton she took a left and headed toward Trinity College, with its spear-like iron gate and somber stone walls. There was a bus stop there. She could board the bus and get away.

Allison Mary Oberon, ya can't get away from me.

She heard her mother's voice as if she were right behind her in the jostling street. Allison turned around, half expecting to see the ghost of Miriam, hands on her hips, cigarette hanging from her slack lips, eyes glinting. But of course she wasn't to be found in the crowd of dark clad people. *Miriam is dead, you idiot,* she chided herself. Still, she found herself hurrying toward the bus stop. The heel of her right shoe caught on the curb of the cobbled street, and she pitched forward.

Such a clumsy one, you. Always trippin' on your own big feet.

Allison felt large arms lift her to her feet, and she looked up into the beefy face of a man with blurred green eyes. For a second, she felt warm and protected, like she used to when Clain held her in the night after one of her spells. Or when her father rocked her to sleep when she was three, before he left her and her mum.

But then the man with the beefy face pulled her to him. He leaned down and smothered her mouth with his, forcing his rough tongue into her. She could taste the stale Guinness in his mouth, and felt the barbs of his stubbly beard. Every nerve in her body hummed with high-pitched terror. She clawed at his eyes with her nails, screaming when he wrenched backward and freed her.

"What th'fuck!" The drunk man turned, and to the by-standers who gawked, proclaimed with a shrug, "She comes on t'me and gives me th'eye, now, and then screams bloody hell. Howd'ya figure that? Crazy bitch, that one."

But Allison was already running for the bus. Just let her, please God, get on that bus and ride forever. Forever riding, never stopping, never thinking, or hearing, or listening to them again. On a bus, she could leave them all behind her, the voices. Always the voices in her head.

She kept her head down, her shoulders hunched, and hands in the pockets of her thin raincoat. She kept walking until she reached the austere spires of Trinity. A few meters from that, she spied the yellow pole of the City Tour bus stop. Allison hugged the pole when she reached it, as if it would disappear if she let go. It might, she thought. It might just disappear, like everything else safe and solid disappears.

But as Allison saw the familiar yellow and green bus round the curve, she relaxed her grip. It pulled up and stopped. Allison dug the euros out of her pocket, and care-fully deposited them into the open hand of the bus driver. He had on a uniform, and a cap with a stiff bill. That's lovely, she thought, people in uniforms can be trusted. You can trust them not to hurt you, or leave you when you're lost or in trouble.

"Can I sit on top?" Allison asked the man. Did she sound too timid?

Must'n be timid, girl, one of the voices said. *Must be assertive. Take up for yourself.*

"I mean ta say, I'll be sitting up top. I'll be takin' the air."

"Sure you can do whatever you like," the guide said, and added a practiced smile as an afterthought.

That's me girl. Show 'em your stuffin'.

Allison grasped the rail of the winding stair and stepped confidently up into the open-air. Buoyed by the words within her, Allison felt warm inside despite the wind that stirred her hair and nipped at her collar when the bus started down the road again. That voice always looked after her, kept her going when she desperately wanted to quit. Was that her father? But no, he'd left her and Miriam when she was only four.

She shook her head and mumbled to herself, something she'd done in secret as a child, but took to doing more and more openly of late. She knew she shouldn't talk out loud to the voices, but she couldn't help it now. The only way to stop them was to talk back. Then they'd be quiet.

Clain was happier when the voices were quiet. And she desperately wanted to make Clain happy, because he'd been good to her—he had. He'd taken her in, let her live with him. She felt so safe, so…content with him. He helped her get the job at J. Grogan's, a respectable pub on South William Street, just down from the Westbury Hotel, where he worked. Allison waited tables for Tommy at the cheerful little pub. She cleaned up after people left, sponging the old wooden table tops inside until they gleamed. The only problem was when she had to clean the chrome café tables outside—the ones with the prism patterns on the top. The shapes caught the weak sun. They radiated waves of light that confused and bothered her, and invited the voices to talk. On sunny days, she would close her eyes as she swabbed the tables. Other than that, she dedicated herself to her job, wiping, sweeping, cleaning and washing fastidiously. She had to…the other voice in her head would not let her do otherwise.

Yer a lazy one, it nagged her, *you've missed a spot, just there. I'll whip you're ass good and long if you don't get up every crumb. I swear I will, girl.*

"You're the tidiest worker we've ever had here," Mr. Malone told her once, and when she'd blushed with pride, he said, "Oh look here, mates. Little Allison is blushing— look at the red cheeks on the girl!"

So uplifted by his praise she was, till she felt as if she were a balloon, filled to bursting—a blushing balloon. She almost floated down the street as she raced for the bus home to tell Clain.

The wind stung her cheeks on the tour bus now and brought her 'round. Vaguely she'd heard the tour guide announce stop number five. A pregnant lady and her blonde child boarded the bus and clamored up the stairs to the top. They sat just in front of her. The little girl took to Allison, turning to look shyly 'round at her. Whenever Allison smiled back, the little one buried her doll face into her mother's bosom.

"Stop six," the tour guide said into a microphone. "The Natural History Museum, or the 'Dead Zoo' as it's called, because of the stuffed animals on exhibit there," he continued in his rehearsed speech.

This arrested the peek-a-boo game she was playing with the child. The phrase rolled around inside Allison's head...*Dead Zoo, Dead Zoo, Dead Zoo.*

The bad voice whispered to her, *I'd like to stuff you, you little cockroach, scuttlin' around under me feet all day. Come back here, and I'll teach you what's for.*

Allison clamped her hands over her ears. She wanted to scream, but they told her never to scream in public, don't make a sound, act nice, sit quiet. She screamed in her mind instead, stop it, stop it, stop it! I don't belong in there! I'm not dead, you can't stuff me. You're the dead one—you belong in the Dead Zoo!

Hah! the good voice retorted, *Don't let that old woman scare ya, luv. She couldn't catch ya anyway, she can barely stand up as 'tis. Don't pay her no mind.*

Despite the good voice cheering her on, Allison's limbs felt rubbery. Her gut felt like she'd swallowed rocks, which were tumbling around with every bump on the road. It will pass, it always passes, she told herself. But more and more it didn't pass, this feeling of being swept away by some current of darkness. Helpless to fight it, longing to quit struggling against its strong pull, some force within her, some remnant of survival, would tug at what must be her soul, and she'd be free of its grip—for awhile.

But it always came back, clutching at her again and again.

"Never, never, never quit," she said aloud.

"Pardon me?" The pregnant lady in the seat ahead of her turned half-way 'round. The woman smiled. Her teeth were white and even. Allison was sure the thought of hurting her children would never occur to her.

Allison's face burned. "Sorry," she explained. "'Never, never, never quit'. Sir Winston Churchill said it—my boyfriend—my *fiancé*—told me so."

The girl Allison had been playing with smiled coyly and stuck her thumb in her mouth. She leaned against her mum. The pregnant lady laughed and said, "Well, it certainly sounds as if you've a fine fiancé. When are you to be married, if I may ask?"

"Oh, in just a little while, now," Allison said. "I've already been shopping, and I've found a lovely dress. It's in the shop window, at Fran and Jane's. Next to the Westbury Mall, you know."

"Oh, the Westbury Mall. *Such* nice shops. I'm sure it's lovely, then." She whispered to her little one, "That lady is going to be a bride, Mara. Like your dolly. Won't she be a sight to see?"

Allison straightened up and smiled at the child, who looked at her with eyes round as saucers.

"A bride with a beautiful white gown to the floor? Really, mummy?"

Allison felt as if she were floating again, on this heady cloud of attention—wonderful, benign attention.

"Oh yes, I'm going to wear a beautiful dress, creamy as

vanilla pudding, it is, with sparkles all over it, and a long train, just like Princess Diana," she said breathlessly. "And the wedding cake'll be strawberry with cream icing thick as snow, don't ya know; with fresh strawberries on top."

"Ooooh, mummy! Just think!" the girl said, and ducked her head again.

"Stop number twelve. St. Patrick's Cathedral," the guide continued, his accent laid on thick for the tourists. "Jonathan Swift it is buried here, with his lady luv, Esther Johnson. Together forever, as they say."

They turned to look at the majestic cathedral, with its spires and lacy, arched windows. Allison thought St. Patrick's looked like an enormous castle of sand, the kind she always dreamed the children of rich English parents built at the seashore in summer. Why, she and Clain could be married right here, at St. Patrick's. Why not? Who's to stop them? She would have to suggest it to him when she got home. Allison was sure he would take to the idea. He was good to her. Even indulged her a bit, if you will. She would waltz down the isle in her creamy dress, long train flowing behind, her cheeks flushed with love...

"Dublin castle to your right." Allison realized the tour guide was still droning on. "Built by the Vikings in Ten-Thirty-Eight. Did ya know now, the Vikings were the ones that named the city. They called the dark water where the River Liffey and the River Poddle join the 'Black Pool'. The Viking word for 'black' was 'dubh' and the word for 'pool' was 'lin', so—there ya have it, Dubh-lin. Dublin."

Black pool, black pool, black pool, the voices whispered.

She shook her head and muttered softly, "No, I won't go. I'm getting married. He loves me."

"...And here you see the oldest church in Dublin," the guide went on, "St. Avians, which was once inside the original stone walls built completely around the city, a segment of which ya can see to your left."

This church did not remind Allison of weddings and christenings. With its dark, looming spikes and rough walls, it reminded her of fortresses, barbarians, battles...death. The sun went behind a cloud, as if to say, *yes, death.*

Allison shut her eyes tight, so that Death could not get in.

"And here," the guide said into the tinny loudspeaker, "is the most popular stop on the Dublin tour. The Guinness factory..." He went on to list dates and facts and how many pints produced per year, but Allison could not hear him for the voices had returned with a vengeance.

Who are you callin' a drunken whore, ya bastard! And why d'ya think I'm after a drink all the time, anyway, huh? It's this girl, here, that you saddled me with. She's ruined me life, she has, making me nervous with all her whinin' and snifflin' and such.

"And on the right here, behind the wall, is St. Patrick's Hospital, a facility for the mentally ill, and those with alcohol-related diseases. As they say, only in Ireland will ya find a hospital for alcoholics just down the road from the Guinness factory. As Jonathan Swift is reported to have said, 'Dublin is the largest open-air asylum in Europe.'"

There were guffaws from the tourists on the bus. The guide was in fine fettle and the crowd loved it. Allison felt the pebbles in her stomach rattle. This was not freedom, or escape. She looked around her at the bloated foreigners with their cameras and their sunglasses that cost more than she made in a week.

Ah, girl, maybe there is no escape.

There *is*. I'm getting married. I've found me love, she argued back.

Have ya now?

"The King's Bridge on your right, built in 1821 to commemorate the visit of King George..."

Allison's eyes barely touched on the handsome white and gold gilt bridge spanning the river, so absorbed was she in observing a mother and her daughter on the walkway below. The sobbing girl, in blue school uniform, held a red balloon in her right hand. Her mother was yanking her by the left, hurrying her along. The girl must've been bad, Allison supposed, to make her mother so angry.

And after I've gone and bought you that lovely balloon. What a bad girl y'are now. You should have a spanking instead of a balloon.

The nice pregnant lady and her child were rising from the seat in front of her. Allison must've been listening to the voices for some time, for they were now in Phoenix park at the Dublin Zoo.

"Best wishes to you on your wedding," the lady said, and the little girl twittered gaily.

"Mum's taking me to the zoo," the little one said as she took her mother's hand.

Allison watched them walk down the curved stairway of the bus. Her eyes followed them down the walk and through the gates of the zoo. She watched until the bus started again with a squeal, until their pale blonde heads disappeared into the crowd.

Something as weightless as a breath evaporated from her and followed them.

"You need help, Allison," Clain had said that morning. "Serious, professional help. I can't do it any more, Allie. I've tried me best, but this thing is too much for you ta handle—it's too much for me ta handle."

"Clain, what are ya tellin' me then?" She felt her palms turn up in a pleading gesture and tried to find his eyes, to read his eyes.

He dropped his head and shook it slowly. His shoulders lifted and then sagged.

"You'll have to go, you know. I'm sorry...in a way, it's me own fault for thinkin' I could fix your problems. Could help ya. There's just too many bad things have happened t'ya that can't be erased—at least, not by me."

"But you do help me, Clain. Baby..." she heard her voice rise and crack. "I can change, I *will* change, oh I'll do anythin' ya say, only don't leave me, oh darlin' Clain, you can't leave me—" he was walking away. She had to stop him. Allison grabbed his thick arm, and felt the muscle contract hard as he pushed her away from him. She fell backward, off the curb in front of the Westbury, in front of all the fine people in their fine clothes.

"Go on, get up now. Do yourself a favor," he said softly, "and go to a hospital. God knows ya need some help before ya kill yourself."

She managed to stand. Her stockings were torn and wide white stripes started running the length of her legs. She stared at the palms of her hands. There was blood oozing red from the scrapes.

Clain had already straightened his uniform. The front doors of the hotel slid open with a whisper. He turned to her before he went in.

"I never loved you, ya know that? I never meant to hurt ya, but I can't take ya on to raise, girl. I've got me own life." He added, as an afterthought, "Sorry, luv. Best of luck, eh?"

Your own da wouldn't have anythin' ta do wit you either. You run him off, you did, and now he's left us. He's left me...alone with you!

Allison turned in her bus seat and sat quietly. The tourists, now anxious for their five o'clock ales, were getting rowdy. She watched as Dublin slid by: the dark waters of the Liffey, Smithfield Village, the Four Courts, the Clarence Hotel, the O'Connell Bridge. Then, out of the corner of her eye, she saw a spot of red in the murky green river. She leaned on the bus rail.

"Look," someone behind her said, "there's a balloon in the river."

There it was. A wilted red balloon drifted in the river toward the bridge.

Ah, girl, maybe there is no escape.

"Stop number nineteen—O'Connell Bridge and Temple Bar." The guide had barely begun the announcement when Allison rushed from her seat and down the stairs.

Once off the bus, she ran in front of it, causing the glib tour guide to curse at her as she hurried across to the bridge.

She could just see the forlorn speck of red as, caught in the rushing current, it disappeared.

❧

Carolyn and I headed into Adare Village to find inspiration for our second piece. Enroute, we came to a big black gate and an adjacent "No Exit" sign. I stopped; Carolyn kept going. That contrast triggered my lifelong push/pull of playing by the rules.

When I presented that conflict as the idea for an essay, Liz suggested I explore why the rules had worked for me and why I was questioning them now. In answering those questions, I traveled farther than the distance from South Carolina to Ireland, confronting on foreign soil a blessing and a curse I'd carried with me all my life.

HANDOUTS AND HANGUPS

by Lucie Barron Eggleston

Playing by the rules has made me safe, sane, and stuck.

So like the good Girl Scout I was brought up to be, I relaxed when I saw handouts in the folder. I had come to the Maui Writers Conference Ireland Retreat to answer the nagging question: "Should I explore writing fiction? Is there any potential at all?" I was excited about the journey. I *wanted* to push myself. However, I still wanted a safety net, and the handout on "The Art of the Short Story" gave me one.

According to the handout, conflict is required "in every scene." I no longer felt safe. *Every* scene? It got worse. "The short story is comprised of three acts: Act One: the Setup, Act Two: the Complication, and Act Three: the Resolution." Furthermore, the handout specified I was to give my characters—who had yet to be conceived—"passion, memorable names, quirks, angers, frustrations, and depth." There was no way I could do all of that—possibly ever—but definitely not by 2:30 the next afternoon.

Later in the lobby of the Westbury Hotel, fellow writer Carolyn Buchanan overheard me talking and approached. "This sounds serious," she said.

"It is," I said. "I just read the handout on 'The Art of the Short Story,' and I'm not at all sure I can do this."

"Rule number one: Don't read the handout," she advised.

What?? Not read the handout? That was no option. Handouts, guidelines, and rules were my friends. Besides, Carolyn just didn't understand. I had to play by the rules…even when they stopped me in my tracks.

Like my junior year in college when I took the speed reading course. Halfway through the six-week course, the instructor asked me to stay for a moment after class. I had been expecting this. "Miss Barron," she began, tight lipped and nasal. "I'm a little worried. You are the only one in the group whose speed has *decreased* since the beginning of the program."

Of course she was upset. I was that awful statistic that didn't respond to the techniques. I was choosing between comprehension and speed. In frantically trying to follow her rules, I was missing the reason for using her system in the first place. Her techniques had failed us both.

Before I had my thyroid gland ablated, I read the yellow Patient Information Sheet six times. I learned that while the radiation was destroying most of my thyroid, I would also be emitting radiation, thus endangering anyone in certain proximity. The safest thing, I concluded, was to send my loved ones away.

The procedure was simple. I was escorted to a room the size of a closet, presented with a thick steel container that housed a separate container that housed the pill. A man in a white lab coat told me to take the pill after he left the room. I did exactly as he said.

Shortly thereafter I exited the building through a long white tunnel, got in my car, and drove home to my 72 hours of solitary confinement. I followed all of the rules: I ate on paper plates that I then put in thick plastic garbage bags. I opened the door for no one. I settled back to watch Julia Roberts in *Step Mom*, the first of my many movies. I had chosen this one because I thought it was a comedy.

Wrong! In less than thirty minutes, the tears started welling, *radioactive* tears, no less, and not one tissue within reach. Furthermore, two specific points on the Patient Information

Sheet flashed in my memory: flush all used tissues down the toilet, and flush the toilet four times after each use.

The pattern formed quickly. I'd watch the movie for five minutes or less, stop the movie, honk radioactive substances into the tissue, run upstairs to the bathroom, drop the contaminated tissue into the toilet, flush four times, return to the den, pick up the remote, and resume the movie and the sobbing.

The thyroid ablation was successful, but the procedure was hard on our plumbing. In retrospect, I acknowledge my response to the instructions was over the top. But to my way of thinking, I was simply following the rules.

When I was growing up, my mother had a fundamental principle that became the primary rule of my life: "Always do your best," she said, and on the surface, who can argue with that? For years I never even tried to, but eventually two questions surfaced. Question #1: Can we ever know what our best is and therefore know we have met expectations? And Question #2: Will my best—and therefore will I—ever be good enough?

Early on I must have sought and found refuge in the rules. Rules turned the nebulous "best" into something more tangible. If I met the expectations set forth in the rules, I might get the approval I sought and needed.

However, there were problems. For one, I believed there would be a payoff—if not immediately, surely ultimately. Experience confirms otherwise. I see "Right Lane Closed Ahead," follow the flashing highway arrow into the left lane, and watch others speeding by me on the right. Apparently those drivers always get where they're going ahead of me. People who can break the rules also seem to have more fun…like the dogs in the alley instead of the well-bred puppies in the pet shop window. I've always been a little envious and somewhat in awe.

For a long time now, I've let the rules dictate how well I measure up. This system breaks down when I encounter rules I don't fully understand or ones I understand but feel incapable of following like "The Art of the Short Story." Then I get stuck.

I came to Ireland to experiment and discover whether there was a fiction writer in me just dying to come out. On purpose, I put myself in a position of being anything but my best. I sat down at the computer. Chris had told our group to "have fun," and Carolyn had said, "Don't read the handout." I began struggling for and with the words. Sometime between midnight and 1 a.m., I gave in. The handout was on the bed. I doubted my story had three purposeful acts, and I knew the characters were low on "quirks, angers, and frustrations," but I wondered where I was in the realm of the required number of words. "A short story is a piece of fiction under 15,000 words," stated the handout. Now I'm no numbers person, but something told me my piece of fiction was nowhere close. I hit "Tools" then "Word Count." My heart sank: 470!

Even though 15,000 words was not the goal for this assignment, I knew I had to do better than 470. I started following my instincts, inserting dialogue and the place I wanted my characters to be by the end of the story. I pressed "Word Count" again: 980! "Good job," I told myself. "It's no finished piece, but it's a solid start."

Rules have their place. They give us guidelines and warnings and standards and protection. They clarify expectations and honor freedom by setting limits. They keep us from hurting ourselves and others more than we already do. But they can't do any of that without our permission. We're the ones who make them, follow them, bend them, and break them.

Following the handout won't write your story any more than watching a green light will get you across the street. You have to step out there, but in all fairness, you're usually better off crossing when the light is green.

There was a way to increase my reading speed without losing my comprehension. With my family away, I didn't have to flush the toilet every time I blew my nose, and one or two flushes would have done the job without putting anyone at risk. And when you get right down to it, "setup, complication, and resolution" are literary terms for "beginning, middle, and end."

I don't want to abandon the rules; I need them too much. We all do. I just want to stop surrendering to them when I need to trust myself. I'm no finished work, but I've gotten a solid start. If I keep at it, who I am and what I have to say will be good enough.

A long walk in the Burren followed by a nice bowl of hot soup in a village pub brought this old tale to mind....

No Pain, Dairee

by Elizabeth George

To get a true grasp on the significance of the incredible walk that I took in the Burren, what you have to understand first is what happens to an unbeliever when she fails to kiss the Blarney Stone in the manner in which it is meant to be kissed. Kissing the stone requires one to engage in a feat that, for someone like myself—terrified of heights to the point of hysteria—is entirely unthinkable. For the kisser is asked to bend over backwards at a great height while trusted individuals hold onto her legs, thighs, knees, ankles, big toes or whatever in order to keep her from toppling over the side of Blarney Castle. Held in this position, she must then place her lips on the sacred stone, from which moment on she is supposed to have the gift of a silver tongue. But if she does not bend backward to kiss the stone, if she bends forward, or blows a kiss at it, or if she slaps a kiss upon it by means of her hand or her fingers, then what happens to the tongue is something quite different, as I found out.

I was warned of this, but I paid no heed. I was too afraid to bend backward and certainly I trusted no one to hold me in place, so when I paid my visit to Blarney Castle, I bent forward instead to get a good grip on the wall and I kissed the stone that way and waited to see what would happen. The wind was blowing fiercely as it tends to do at the top of Blarney Castle (and all over the rest of Ireland, if it comes down to it) and the moment I kissed the stone the wrong way, a thunderous crash rent the heavens and it began to rain. I dashed for cover. I laughed and said, "So that was it? A bit of thunder? A bit of rain? Well, I'm afraid of neither." From that moment on, I gave no further thought to the stone or how I had kissed it.

I went from Blarney to the Ring of Kerry, and from the Ring I traveled north to an area called The Burren. This is a landscape like no other, one hundred square miles of limestone plateau, a place of caves, of mysterious lakes that appear one day and disappear the next, of delicate wildflowers seen in no other spot in Europe, of cows and sheep grazing placidly where there are stony pastures for them, of prehistoric cairns and villages, of ancient cottages and tumbling churches and graveyards left to fend for themselves in the harsh weather that comes right off the Atlantic.

I stayed in a hotel where I had been a guest twenty-six years earlier, a lovely old place that sits between the villages of Lisdoonvarna and Ballyvaughan. The drive from Kerry took me the entire day, and when I arrived, I was bone weary and eager to sample something from the hotel bar that might revive me. My usual drink is gin and tonic, and that's what I had. My choice of this over a Guinness—or even a Smithwick's—caught the attention of a gentleman who was having a late afternoon pint of stout. He was struck by my lack of adventure, I suppose, or perhaps it was the fact that I hadn't even ordered Irish gin, if there is such a creature.

He said, "What'll y'be drinking that nonsense f'r when y'can have a real bit of Irish brew of the likes you won't get where you come from?"

I hadn't the heart to tell him that I don't like Guinness. A Smithwick's doesn't go down badly, but when push comes to shove, there's really nothing like a gin and tonic to put one's life back into perspective. I asked him what he liked about Guinness. He said, "Where're you from then, lady?"

I said, "Is it the accent, then?"

To which he replied, "Ha! No. It's the bloody stupidity of the question."

I was rather miffed as I'd only been trying to make conversation, and I suppose he saw that he'd ruffled my feathers. He introduced himself as Seamus O'Rourke and I took his measure as unobtrusively as I could manage.

Truth is, he looked like someone out of central casting. The call had gone out for Typical Irishman to Amuse American Tourists, and Seamus O'Rourke got sent for the part. Top to toe, he was a man of the sod, and he was carrying a good deal of it on his green Wellingtons. Above them, the knees of his faded jeans were worn, as was his cardigan. This was unbuttoned, for the hotel's bar kept a peat fire burning from noon until late night so it was warm within, and beneath this cardigan was what the Irish call a grandfather shirt of cream striped in green—five buttons, no collar, and soft from myriad washings.

Seamus—for so he asked to be called—said, "I c'n see I've overstepped myself, dear lady, so I'd like to make it up to you."

I said, "No worries. No making up is necessary."

"But this is Ireland," he said, "where the stranger is welcome."

He went on to tell me that although he was a farmer just up the road—dairy cows, he informed me, although from the scent of him, I didn't need to be told—he had a sideline in walks in the Burren. He usually charged for this: thirty euro a head, including lunch. But in my case and as I was a lovely lady and as he'd quite overstepped himself...Could he take me out onto the Burren for a look at the flowers? With May, they were blooming like the dickens. No mere furze out there, he told me. This was the real stuff: from gentians to orchids. But if I wanted to see them, I would need an Irishman to tell me what was what.

This sounded like a line, but I liked the look of him. Forty years old, I guessed. He was rough around the edges but I expected he might clean up well. Not that I was looking, naturally. But a walk in the Burren with an Irishman who knew the routes and could name the flowers...It sounded like an interesting diversion.

We set a time: ten o'clock the next morning. "And be well rested," Seamus warned me. "If we're going to walk, we're going to *walk*. Alone, are you? Husband, companion, children with you?"

No, I was alone, I said.

He winked and said, "Good. You'll see some sights you've

never thought to see before the day is done."

These were prescient words, as I would discover.

The next morning dawned misty, but I was not put off by this. I'd brought rain clothes and walking shoes, and at 10:00 a.m. exactly I presented myself at the door to the hotel. There Seamus was, dressed as before but this time with a great waxed jacket and a rucksack as well. "Lunch," he told me. When he picked it up, I heard the *clink* of bottles. I had a good idea of what lunch would be.

We set off by car, for in the immediate area of the hotel the Burren can be seen but not immediately accessed. We drove north, through Ballyvaughan and out onto the coastal road. We were going to Fanore, Seamus told me. A green road there led into the hills and from there the Burren Walk climbed to a peak from which the Aran Islands could be viewed. It was a bit of a drive, but it wouldn't take long. I should relax and enjoy the scenery.

Seamus drove along the coast in a fury, which I had come to understand was typical driving for Irishmen of a certain age or under certain conditions. He seemed sober as a stone, so I assumed it was the of-a-certain-age kind of driving I'd seen on my own drive from the south. We careened around the curves in the road and passed slower cars with unthinking abandon. In no time we were in Fanore, making a turn towards St. Patrick's Church, along a route that was apparently referred to by the locals as Khyber's Pass. It followed the course of a tumbling, rock-strewn river and soon enough forked. We went to the right and within fifty yards came to a rough area of stones and dirt that gave way to one branch of the Burren Walk, which curved up the hill. There we parked.

Seamus said, "So. Come along. You want flowers and there are flowers to make you weep and bless Jesus."

I didn't point out that I hadn't wanted flowers, that he had invited me as a form of apology. I merely followed, grateful that I was in good condition for scrambling up a stony path, thankful that I'd brought an old pair of walking shoes with me, shoes that could bear the mud and the cow manure that graced our route.

Alas. Seamus, it must be said, was not much of a guide. He occasionally crooked his finger and barked, "Cow parsley," or "Gentian over there," or "Cornflowers" or "Orchids, c'n you credit it?" And the pace he set was ruthless. There was no time for pictures or anything else. A glance at the blooms was obviously supposed to be sufficient.

In this manner of death march, we came to the crest of the hill. Seamus paused, and for a moment I thought we were meant to rest. But Seamus—although stationary for the first time in the hike—was neither pausing for breath or to admire the view. Instead, his eyes were fixed on a lone, white, tumble-down cottage set in a high pasture studded with limestone. A chimney on this cottage sent a plume of smoke upwards. The smell of sod burning was unmistakable: acrid and welcoming at the same time.

To my surprise, Seamus set off for this cottage without a word of explanation. I followed in his wake. I noticed that there was a smaller, secondary building nearby and remembering the *clink* I'd heard from Seamus's rucksack, I wondered....It would be a real adventure, I thought. Here I am in the Burren with an Irishman, and we're about to buy some of the old poteen.

As we got close, the cottage door opened. Another character from Central Casting appeared. This one was standing in the role of Old Irish Crone. As you would expect, she was in black from head to toe and when she spoke, I saw that a good many of her teeth were missing.

"G't in, g't with you," she said. "There's rain to come and rain to go. G't in, for you've walked a pace so far this marning, haven't ye?"

Seamus urged me forward and as the old crone called him by name, I decided it was safe enough. I found myself in a stone-floored cottage of three rooms only: a central one that served as kitchen and sitting room—if two wobbly chairs, a rocker, and an old settle can be called a sitting room—and two others with rough-hewn doors that were closed.

"Bide a bit and have some soup," the old crone said. She

brought forth soda bread fresh from the kettle and made in the old way: with fiery hot sod piled on the lid and the kettle itself sitting close to the fire. And from another bigger kettle she ladled soup into an earthenware bowl.

The bread was fragrant as only soda bread can be, and I was seduced by the smell. I took a piece and, because she was so eager to please and because I didn't want to offend her, I took the soup as well. For his part, Seamus took nothing from her, and he didn't seem offended that I chose to eat her food and not his own. He brought forth a massive sandwich from his rucksack, and he ate heartily, also drinking the two bottles of Guinness he'd brought with him.

I'd finished my soup when a terrible cry came from one of the other two rooms. Seamus stirred and seemed likely to rise. The old woman waved him down and otherwise ignored it. She smiled at me and said, "Good that, innit," and she nodded at my bowl which was completely empty. "You eat a fair good one," she told me. I didn't know what she meant, but when she offered me more, I refused with thanks. My reason had more to do with wanting to be gone than with being sated, for another cry and then another came from the nearest of the rooms.

Seamus stood abruptly. He said, "We'll be off."

I gestured to my purse, "Should I...?" For the old woman was obviously poor as dirt and she'd fed me generously and no doubt could use the money.

He shook his head. "Twill offend," he murmured. "We best be off. Now. No tarrying further."

As he spoke, the door to the crying room opened, and a greatly pregnant woman stood there. She was panting like a horse at the end of the race and she was all sweat. She cried out, "Please! Please!" which was when Seamus took my arm and hustled me from the place. Things were looking unpleasant, and I had no problem with being hustled.

I had time to hear the Old Crone murmur, "Come, come, dairee, things do pass," before Seamus had me outside and was hauling me up the slope of the pasture towards the Burren Walk again.

I said, "Who is she? Do you know her? Is she a midwife? Why would someone come out here, of all places...? Seamus, wait. *Wait.*"

But waiting was the last thing he wanted to do. He walked like a man pursued by the devil. And so did I, for the first quarter hour.

Then a pain hit me like a sword through my stomach. It traveled down in a blast of burning coal and it clenched me so hard I doubled over. I cried out and knew at once that I'd eaten something foul, something putrid, something my body was warring against. I felt horrible, on the edge of death, and I knew what it was. For I'd felt this way once before, at the hands of a *croque monsieur* in France. Then I'd been ill for a ghastly sixteen hours as my system tried to purge from itself ham gone very very bad.

The soup hadn't been broth. It had been creamy with cooked- down ingredients, but as to what they were, I had no blessed idea.

I thought how stupid I had been, and I called out to Seamus another time. He stopped. I was doubled over, mindless of the mud and the stone by now, mindless of rain that had begun to fall. I was clenched by spasms that made me shriek. "Ambulance," I said hoarsely. "Doctor. Help."

Seamus squatted by me. "What the *devil*...? What's happened? Damn, you shouldna ate what she offered. Did you see me eat it? Did you? Did you? Bah, you tourists!"

"But you didn't say..." I could talk no more. I knew I was going to die in the Burren. I was going to die like a dog, there in the mud. I clawed at this. I grabbed onto to the grass that grew on the edge of the path. I howled and I shrieked.

This went on for two hours. And during this time, though I wept and pleaded, Seamus did nothing to help me. He hunkered next to me and looked concerned and occasionally patted me on the back. But that was it. As for me, I cursed the man and I cursed his children and grandchildren in one direction and all of his ancestors in the other. And I cursed myself for the fool I was to go walking with a stranger in the limestone Burren. When I wasn't cursing, I was praying.

Never have I known such unrelieved pain and unrelieved fright.

And then, it passed. As it had come, so it went. But I was spent, and I couldn't think how I would ever get down from the Burren.

Seamus helped me to my feet. He put his sturdy arm around my waist—and wasn't *that* the limit of the help he gave me?—and slowly we made our way down the hill. But at the pasture where the cottage stood, he stopped. Smoke still came from the chimney, and the door was cracked open.

"I'll have a word," Seamus said, and he sounded as if he meant business.

I said, "No. Forget it. Please. I just want to get to the hotel." And sleep, I thought. I could do with some sleep.

He said, no, he would have his word and I could wait for him there or come with him to confront the Old Crone. It was all the same to him. But as it looked like more rain to come—

And the heavens opened again at that, quite as if Seamus had a direct line to Mother Nature.

I said I'd go with him. So we stumbled through the pasture once more, and when we reached the cottage, Seamus swung the door open.

The Old Crone was not in evidence in the cottage's main room, but the room wasn't empty. A woman sat in the creaking rocking chair next to the fire and in her arms she held a baby. She was nursing this infant and when she looked up, I saw it was the woman we had seen earlier, the one who had been greatly pregnant. Which she no longer was.

She said, "A boy, Seamus O'Rourke. It was as she said. So quick. No pain. And we have a son."

We. I looked from Seamus to the woman to Seamus again. Behind him, the door of the second room opened. There stood the Crone while behind her on the bed, another woman lay. She writhed and she panted and she moaned.

"No pain, dairee," the old woman said to her just before she closed the door. "You shall see like your sister. No pain atall."

Then she smiled at me. She said, "You bin a far long walk. Takes strength f'r that. You be wanting more soup."

She went to the fire where the kettle still boiled. She reached for a ladle and an earthen bowl.

But I was out of the door of the cottage before she had another bowl of soup dished up to offer me. I ran down the hill and from there to the car and from there to the coastal road. I didn't stop running till I reached the hotel, despite it being thirteen miles away. And when I arrived, I had a Guinness for regret, and I swore I'd not talk to any Irishmen, living or dead, ever again.*

So that's the story of what happened to me when I went into the Burren with Seamus O'Rourke. And if you believed even a word of it, I have a bridge for sale that I'd like to show you.

For here's what happens when you kiss the Blarney Stone in a way that you oughtn't: Your tongue becomes silver just as you hoped, but every word you utter is a bloody lie.

*Adapted with massive additions from an old Irish lie heard on the radio years ago.

*The striking red doors of St. Anne's church in Dublin cap-
tured me from the moment I saw them. They seemed so out of place
on a church, like Betty Davis in □Jezebel wearing a red dress when
she should have been in mourning black. After that, it was a matter of finding the right sin to go with those crimson doors.*

Sign Language
by John Tullius

I never could read signs. Not like some people who can
tell by the change of a woman's perfume that she's ready to
walk out on you. I mean I can pick up on stuff like smoke
before fire and dark clouds before rain—but seeing that my
world was about to crash in on me? Never.

But even I should have seen the neon pulse of God's sign
language that morning in Dublin. The double red doors of
St. Anne's Church, the red lights flashing in rhythm with the
sirens of the ambulance weaving its way up Grafton Street,
her blood spreading in a crimson pool across the pavement.

As usual, I thought I'd outsmarted everyone. I was good
at that—outsmarting everyone, including myself. I'd been
bringing Diane along on these trips for years, putting her up
in the hotel on another floor, then when my wife and daughter were out shopping or in a jet-lag swoon, I'd sneak down
to her room. She was in our group of aspiring writers and
we joked about all the tutoring I was giving her, the hours of
grueling well-someone's-got-to-do-it foreplay, the
lovemaking intensified by the sneaking around, the excuses,
the signals (slowly sliding her painted fingernail across her
lips) at a crowded dinner table.

Di joined our writing group five years ago. We'd meet
once a week and critique each other's work, offer encouragement, and bitch about the money hungry whores in the
publishing business at guard, it seemed, against our getting
published. Sometimes we'd go to writers conferences together and once a year my wife Amber and I organized a

trip to someplace like Rome or Paris, someplace filled with history and beauty and inspiration, where we could all write and drink and eat and laugh. And Di and I could make love, of course. This year we had picked the arresting green of Ireland.

We were on the Veneto in Rome when Di and I found ourselves alone for the first time even though we'd been eyeing each other for months. We ended up sharing a bottle of red in Nino's off the Spanish Steps. It was innocent enough until I leaned into her as we laughed about something, a swirl with the intoxication of Rome, and we kissed. It wasn't a show-stopping kiss. It was playful, and in her room later that afternoon we had more fun, innocent fun it seemed. (I always made it very clear that I never wanted anyone to get hurt.) We laughed a lot and had enthusiastic sex and laughed some more.

Diane had a husband who didn't share her passion for writing and she left him conveniently at home for these trips. She moved to a different town soon after Rome and she stopped coming to the weekly meetings (which actually made the relationship even more ideal), but she made it a point to come on our once-a-year sojourns.

It was all innocent fun. Her husband had a yacht and a jet plane and she wasn't leaving that for what we had. (At least that's what she assured me.) And I had a comfortable life and a daughter I adored named Liv, short for Olive, named after my wife's mother, a horrible shrew who told Amber the first chance she got that she didn't trust me.

Liv was my joy, a peripatetic rebel from birth. I joked that when Liv was six months old she wanted to get her own apartment. It wasn't much of an exaggeration. She squirmed in her high chair as an infant and as soon as she could walk and figure out our front door handle, she was off in full two-year-old stride running down the street to God knows where. She always wanted to go. It didn't matter where. And it didn't matter that she was born deaf.

She was in her first year of university now and she still went with us on these trips. She fell in love with Paris and went back there for her sophomore year of high school. Then she spent a year in Japan before entering college just to "see more of the world," signing her way wherever she went, making herself understood by the sheer force of her will, and hers was a ferocious make-way-for-Liv will.

She was the first one to see that there was something up with Diane and I, and she confronted me that bright Irish morning on Dawson Street, across from St. Stephen's Green.

"I don't get why you don't have the guts to leave Mom," she said, her hands whirring off the words for emphasis as she spoke in that yawning voice of the deaf.

"What?" I said, buying time. But Liv never backed off. Never.

"You heard me. Why not just pack it in. You obviously don't love her."

"Of course, I love your mother." I shot back at her, taking an authoritative tone that translated to my hip cocking to one side.

She didn't buy it, shaking her head furiously.

"Oh, so I guess that's why you're fucking Diane Two-face." This she didn't bother to sign. She yelled it as loud as she could, which was like a whisper amplified.

"Hey, watch your language, missy. I'm still your father." I slashed back at her with my forefinger waggling. I also stood straight for effect.

This only made her smile. I'm not sure if it was because I called her missy, like we were watching a repeat of *The Waltons*, or because of the theatrics that I was always so poor at. She looked away for a second still smiling, but when she looked back up at me she was glaring with those ferocious green eyes of hers that had always had the goods on me.

"Just because Mom's too stupid to see it, doesn't mean you're not fuckin' up royal here, Dad." She signed every word but "fuckin' up" and "Dad." She was a genius at sub-text.

I let the words hang in the air for a moment. I'd always been pretty much of a coward and she had pinned me into one of those inescapable corners that a person as spineless as I am can usually squirm his way free of. But not with Liv.

She was a marksman when it came to my heart and she'd stuck me dead center like some bug in a specimen drawer.

"Look," I said, "just because I've had an ...indiscretion, doesn't mean I love you or your mother any less."

The horns began honking furiously down the street behind us but, of course, Liv couldn't hear them and I was busy trying not to lose my grip on her.

I took her hand and she looked at it, then up at me. I thought I could see the sheer weight of her disappointment. I guessed it was that terrible moment we all face when we realize Daddy isn't perfect.

"Oh, Dad," she said, patting my hand and shaking her head wearily. "I've known since I was eight years old that you've been having affairs."

"What are you talking about...." I tried to lie, but she was having no part of that.

"Let's see, there was Dottie What's-her-name. Karen Siskel. Then, that stick that looked like a praying mantis, I forget her name." She was using her fingers to tick them off. Dottie, one finger. Karen, two fingers. The mantis (actually, Kat Deerland), three fingers. Then she held her hands up as if to put a halt to it all.

"You're just never going to stop, are you?"

The honking and commotion had risen to a din and as it got closer I looked up and there was Di at the corner where we had agreed to meet, and across the street was Amber just crossing over. I realized in that instant that Liv had set this whole thing up to force me to confront all of it, all my weakness, my cowardice, my love for her, and my simpering love for her mother.

It was the same instant that I spotted the car careening down Dawson, sideswiping a taxi at one corner, then shooting off toward the opposite sidewalk, tearing out part of the Green's ornate fence, people screaming and scattering, behind the wheel a man completely out of control, braking for nothing, least of all stop signs and red lights and all the other sign language of civilized men, mowing down everything and everyone in his way.

Liv let go of my hand and turned and ran toward Trinity, unaware, of course, of the terrible high-pitched screeching of metallic death hurtling toward us all—Amber on one corner, Di on the opposite, both frozen in horror, and Liv running, forever running, and me shouting, uselessly shouting.

"Liv! Liv! Liv!"

There once was a bugger named Slugger,
Who fell into life as a mugger.
But he couldn't run,
From a man with a gun,
And his famous last words were, "Oh, fugger!"

—Bonnie Christoffersen and Aimée Carter

Being born and raised in the Pacific Northwest where an old building is a hundred, I wanted to see really old things in Ireland. So the first chance I had, I wandered to the old section of Dublin and saw Dublin Castle, Christchurch Cathedral, and the old city wall. It was amazing to me that the ancient walls were still there, mortar and all. What if somebody stole a block of the stone? And why would they steal it? And what would it be like to be from a family with a tradition as old as when the saints walked Ireland over a thousand years ago? Maybe my Irish great-great grandmother would have been able to tell me. But since she died before I was born, I didn't get the chance to ask her. So I took a nap, courtesy of jetlag, and asked my muse instead.

Stone Walls

by Val Ford

Fiona Keegan stood pressed into the arched stone gateway of the old city wall of Dublin. Her cell phone's earbud crackled on the open connection and her hands ached from nearly half an hour of pressing the rumbling drill in her hand against ancient mortar. The arthritis in her middle finger made her grit her teeth and curse her brother Ian for breaking it thirty-five years ago. But she'd have to forgive him after his work tonight.

She looked up the street to where she knew Ian stood leaning against a building, ready to warn her if someone headed her way. Her husband, Tom, stood in the other direction, hidden in a pool of dark that the street lights didn't quite hit. She knew he'd be glowering. None of this was his idea.

"Are you about done?" Tom complained via the cell phone conference call.

"I wish." The frequency of the drill's vibration was slowing and Fiona was afraid that the second Black & Decker battery would wear down before she finished. She'd had to change it when she'd only just started on the longer side of the corner block that she was trying to free. Her arms ached from holding the drill at eye level and rock dust filled her nostrils, blocking the smell of mold and damp stone that permeated the place.

"I can't believe I let you talk me into this," her brother said, but he was laughing a little.

"Why not? It's our brick."

"Shit, Fi, a gardá just turned down my street. I don't think he'll see it that way."

Fiona pulled the drill bit out of the hole and stepped back into the shadow of the gate archway, crouching down.

"Oh, dear god, sis, he's seen you."

Fiona tucked the drill into her backpack and had a sketchpad and a peanut butter and jelly sandwich in her hands when the police car pulled up to the curb.

"Dear God, indeed," Fiona prayed under her breath. She took the earphone out of her ear, slid it into her pocket and then lifted the half-eaten sandwich to her lips, and took a small bite.

The gardá got out, surveying the area as he watched her. He looked middle aged and bored. Well fed.

"Evening, officer." Fiona stood, drawing his eyes with her movement. She'd try to keep it that way. One hand waved her partial sandwich around. "Just taking a little break." She took another bite and made a show of chewing and swallowing before inviting conversation.

He approached, relaxing. "What business brings you here at two in the morning?"

Fiona swallowed again and set her sandwich on top of her pack. "I've been sketching. The Night from the Gates." She lifted her pad to show the half-completed sketch Ian had done for her earlier. She let the pencil slip through her fingers and leaned down to pick it up.

"Nice woman like you shouldn't be out alone this time of night." He was close to her now, standing with the spot Fiona had been drilling to his back. Fiona felt caged in the archway, black iron gate beside her and cold stone behind.

"I'm glad I have a nice policeman like you looking out for me." Fiona hoped he didn't turn or look down at the pile of fresh mortar dust beneath his feet. It was all she could do not to glance over his shoulder. "But I refuse to be ruled by my fear. I moved to America thirty years ago and I've spent the last five years saving up for this trip back home. The daylight washes away the ghosts and I've come to see my great-great grandfather if I can. Legend is he died near here."

The gardá rolled his eyes. "Finish up and head on back to where you're staying. Soon then." He walked back to his car shaking his head.

Fiona picked up her sandwich again and pretended to eat it as he drove away. Her hands were shaking so badly that she ended up pressing them against her chest, smearing peanut butter into her gray shirt.

As the lights disappeared around the corner, Fiona waited, sketchpad in hand. She put the earbud back on.

"I'm back." She announced quietly.

"Don't do anything yet, Fiona," her brother said.

"I wasn't planning on it. I figure he'll go around the block a time or two."

"Sure enough, Fi. I think he's back now," Tom said and soon afterwards lights turned down the street from his direction.

Fiona waved as the gardá drove by slowly.

They all waited a little longer without speaking. And then Tom said, "I know I said I wouldn't help, but screw this. We're finishing now." He jogged the block and a half toward her and took up a chisel and hammer from her pack. Several hard blows along her neatly drilled lines of holes broke the block free. Tom set it into Fiona's outstretched hand and she wrapped it in a sweatshirt and tucked it into her backpack along with the tools.

"Thanks," she said.

"You scared the crap out of me. I hope this thing's worth it."

"Blessings always are," she said and reached out to touch

the line of his jaw. He wasn't pretty in the least, but he was solid and undeniably hers. "Sometimes you amaze me."

"And you me." He grabbed her hand and they walked to where Ian's car was parked. She looked over her shoulder at the little jag in the outline of the gateway in the old city wall. She didn't feel any triumph at the feat, and that worried her.

*

Kathleen Keegan bustled around her condo, getting dinner ready and making sure everything looked good. Her phone rang and her mood lightened as she answered, "Hi, Taunya. Yes, I'm so excited about the wedding… I know, Chris is so gorgeous. I must be the luckiest girl in the world. I'm so glad you introduced us."

Taunya's twins made noise in the background and Kathleen hugged herself. It wouldn't be too much longer and she'd be married with a baby, too. No more drifting along. Taunya still called every day, but it was hard being best friends when they had less and less in common. And it wasn't just Taunya. It seemed like all of her friends were getting husbands and having babies. Or sometimes the other way around. At any rate, they were leaving her behind and alone.

Kathleen made the appropriate noises about the babies' first shots and promised to call in the morning. She checked the clock and figured she had just enough time for a quick shower before Chris arrived.

An hour later, Kathleen sighed silently and pushed the food on her plate around with her fork.

"I can't believe your parents ran off to Ireland. It's only two months before our wedding. You'd think your mom had enough to do here." Chris, her fiancé, set his glass back onto the table. "I've thought about it and I want a formal dinner dance instead of the light buffet reception. It'll be a good chance to invite my dad's friends that I've been trying to recruit. Oh, and I told Stan we'll have drinks with the Taylors on Friday. It's a good thing you didn't go with your parents to Ireland." Chris took a bite of his steak. "This isn't very tender. Where'd you buy it, anyway?"

Kathleen was too tired to bristle. "Safeway. Same place I bought everything else." She looked out the window at the rain obscuring her view of the Willamette River. Only the lights of Portland's bridges broke through the gloom from the rainy evening. "How did your fitting go this afternoon?"

"That was today? Shit." He poured a glug of A-1 onto his plate and dipped a large chunk before devouring it off of his fork. "Oh, before I forget, I got paid today, so here's some money for groceries and whatever. I appreciate you cooking for us all the time." He opened his wallet and passed her several bills which she accepted with a smile.

"Thanks, Chris. About the fitting, I don't suppose your brother went either?"

"How would I know? I wasn't there, remember?" He smiled as he chewed, then he reached over the table and pulled the spaghetti strap from her shoulder. "I was too busy thinking about you."

Kathleen felt her lips curve appropriately. "I'll reschedule for you. Will you call your brother?"

"Better. He wants me to meet him later." He looked at his watch, took a couple last bites and then pushed his plate aside and stood up. "Why don't you come over here and show me again why you want to be Mrs. Knight?"

Kathleen stood and leaned into his kiss, slipping her fingers around his tie and loosening the knot before pulling it off. She tilted her head and tried to direct his lips to the spot on her neck that made her want to drop her skirt, but he was already busy with her zipper.

Later as he dressed and left with a quick kiss and one of his charming smiles, she wandered around her condo cleaning up. When the door closed, she stood in front of her closet, which held the wedding dress that made her look like a princess. She pulled on the corset, lacing it clumsily behind herself before slipping the satin overskirt over the full petticoats. She stared at the vision in the mirror as she put the tiara and veils on, but couldn't bring herself to smile.

♣

Fiona turned the stone block over in her hands. Through

the cracks in the remaining mortar, she'd swear she could see the narrow braid that her ancestor had wrapped around the block when it had originally been set in place. The hair had worn off the face ages ago, leaving only small holes in the edge of the mortar. She shifted to the front edge of Katy's leather couch and held the piece of stone out to her daughter. "I got it for you."

Katy leaned toward Fiona, hand extended, and Fiona's heart pumped in excitement. The first time Fiona had touched the stone set into the wall, it had been like being kissed by an angel on the top of her head. She'd never been the same since. Her own mother had been standing beside her and she'd told Fiona that it had worked and she was glowing. They'd both cried. Happy tears. Holy tears. Tears marking the passing of the saint's blessing on her many-times-great-grandmother.

Katy's fingers closed around the stone. "I can't believe you pried this out of the wall." She looked at the pale tan block, turning it over and over in her hand.

Fiona watched, getting a little worried. "My mother told me that this block holds a blessing of happiness in it for the women in our family. Just before I got married she took me to visit it and told me to come back every day for a week. Since you couldn't come to Ireland, I brought the block to you."

"Are you sure it's the same one?"

"It's got to be the one. Iona —that's our ancestor—gave a saint the meal she'd brought to the wall construction that was supposed to go to her father. Who I bet was mad. And then the saint caught a block that was going to hit Iona on the head and passed it to her with a blessing. Iona cut her hair and wrapped the braid around it and had her father set it into the wall. And then I guess she lived happily ever after."

"Well, that is definitely hair in there."

Fiona frowned. The air around Katy was, if anything, darker. Nothing glowed around her. Fiona's excitement faded and her heart felt like it sank back into her chest.

"You're too good to me, Mom." Katy's smile was brittle. Stressed. Just like the rest of her.

"I just want you to be happy, Katy. It's our tradition. Like the saint said to our ages-ago-grandmother, may the Lord bless you and your daughters with happiness."

Katy held the block up. "I guess it works. I'm happy." Katy didn't quite meet her eyes.

Fiona hated the lie she read in her daughter's face.

"But I don't think you should have brought that here. What if it only works in the wall? What if you made it mad?" Katy said.

"It's a blessing, Katy. I don't think you can screw it up." Fiona felt tears threatening. Something was very wrong.

Katy bowed her head over the stone, eyes closed for a moment. "I think I should give it back to you." Katy set it on the table between them and ran her manicured fingertips over the block. A look of longing crossed her face, too quickly covered up with that strained smile. "I think you should put it back. I don't feel blessed."

"But Katy..."

"Really, Mom. This is scaring me. Promise me you'll take it back as soon as you can. Tomorrow even."

"I can't just go back right now."

"Mom, you have to. I don't like the way it's making me feel."

"Okay. I'll take care of it." Fiona wrapped the stone block back up in her sweatshirt and bustled around, getting her purse together. "I haven't told you this before, but I'm worried about you. You don't seem as happy with Chris as you should be."

"I know what I'm doing, Mom."

"Okay, I'll drop it." Fiona hugged Katy before she left. "I'm sorry, Katy, I love you."

She couldn't get the feeling of blessing and of the angel's kiss she'd received so many years ago out of her head. She sat in her Subaru in the parking lot, praying and listening, waiting for some action to feel right. She unwrapped the brick and prayed and cried, her tears dripping onto the worn stone.

A little before noon she decided to trust the blessing.

She crossed to Katy's car and searched the wheel well for the magnetic key Tom had hidden there. She pulled it off and opened Katy's trunk and stuck the brick in with the spare tire.

Later that night, Fiona couldn't fall sleep. At eleven o'clock she broke down and called Katy, but got voicemail instead.

At eleven fifteen, Chris called, "Fiona, Katy's in surgery here at Legacy. I'm so sorry. We were fighting and I guess I wasn't paying attention the way I should have. I was driving her car and I just lost control and hit the side of the Steel Bridge."

"Hold on just a second." Fiona rasped out as she set the phone down and walked outside and yelled toward the sky. "How could you? It was supposed to be a blessing." She stood in the drizzle for a minute as Tom found her and held her. Then she pulled away and went back to the phone, tears running in a torrent down her face. She had to cough to clear her throat. "What did they tell you? Is she going to be all right?"

"They think so, but she looked pretty bad. Just come. I have to go now. I have to make another call."

Golden warmth flooded Fiona and she nearly dropped the phone as she felt the angel kiss on her head again. "Not yet, Chris. Tell me everything again. It's just starting to sink in." Fiona closed her eyes as the blessing filled her and by the time Chris stopped talking again, she knew what she needed to ask. "Where did they take her car?"

"Her car?"

"Yes, you had it towed?"

"I think it's at A-1."

Fiona made Tom stop on the way and then they spent a long night in the hospital waiting for Katy to get out of surgery. They hugged each other in relief when the doctor told them she would be fine. When Katy was moved into a room, Fiona set a duffle bag holding the brick in her closet.

Kathleen hurt all over. Pain ran like acid through the doughy numbness from the medication.

Kathleen's roommate laughed and hugged her husband and son as they signed her cast. Morphine wasn't the only thing making that woman happy. Kathleen wasn't sure what it was about that woman's husband, but he had spent the morning making his wife and son smile and Kathleen miserable. She wanted what they had. They truly loved being together. She wasn't sorry to see her roommate go home right after lunch.

In the late afternoon, Kathleen watched Chris wave hello from the doorway of the hospital room and weakly raised her hand in reply. He was sorry. Shit. It all hurt.

His story about work went on longer than usual and then he started in on the wedding plans. He wanted to up the dinner to a river cruise. That way no one he wanted to talk with could stay for a few moments after dinner and just slip away. He'd have a chance to make the most of it.

Kathleen reached for her water glass and spilled it.

"God, Kathleen. Let me call the nurse."

"There's a towel in the bathroom."

He pressed the button on the bed's controller. "Don't worry about it, that's why they are here. They can clean up after you."

"You're really a piece of work, you know that, Chris?"

"Just lay back and relax. I'll have them get you a Valium too."

"Like hell you will."

"Do you need something?" The intercom asked.

Chris said, "Yes."

Kathleen said, "No. I'm fine." Their voices intersected. "Chris was just grabbing a towel."

"Call me back if you decide." The intercom turned off.

"I'm not getting it."

"Then get out of here. I don't want to be around somebody who treats people like that."

"It's just a nurse. And if you feel that strongly, I'll get the damn towel." Chris found one in the bathroom and threw it to her on the bed.

"It's not just the nurse." She wiped the table and then dropped the towel in the puddle on the floor. "It's my parents, too. Do you know how many times you've upgraded our wedding reception? They are being so nice. They haven't complained at all."

"But it's a once-in-a-lifetime chance."

"Somehow I think you'll be doing this more than once. Just take this and go." She twisted off her ring and tossed it at him.

The ring landed in the closet and Chris pulled a duffel out, setting it beside her on the bed. Then he picked up the ring and put it in his slacks pocket. "I'll come and see you tomorrow. I hope you feel better then." He tried to slam the door behind himself and had to settle for a slow loud thunk as the mechanism allowed it to close.

"Trust me. This is more than that." Kathleen whispered and unzipped the bag. A warm glow started at the top of her head and flooded down her body. A little while later her doctor came in to see her holding a stone block and crying.

She looked up and tried to smile through her tears. The young doctor in front of her was square and solid all over. And not very pretty. Kathleen liked the look of that.

"Let's see how you're doing," he said and helped her set aside the block and the duffel.

Fiona and Kathleen grinned at each other in the dim light as they smoothed mortar into place around a stone wrapped in a braid made of hair cut from both of their heads. A little while later as they walked to the car where Tom waited, they looked over their shoulders to see the archway of the old city gate of Dublin looming whole and massive in the moonlight. A gardá drove by slowly on the street beside them, but didn't stop. Kathleen wondered how he could have missed seeing her mother glowing in the moonlight. Fiona knew. Blessings are sometimes in disguise.

Storytellers discover secrets in plain view; they open doors be-tween the mundane and the mysterious. At home I write about Iron Age Celts for whom magic was not legend but life. There is a tradition on the Emerald Isle of slipping alone into the ever-present, unseen world and returning with wisdom or madness, and magi-cal gifts. What better place might I follow my senses and intuition to discover doors to story? Musing at thresholds in Ireland led to my inspiration for this essay.

THE DOORS

by Judith Heath

When I arrive in Dublin, I am neither here nor there. The cycles of my body and mind have yet to synchronize with the moon and sun after flying through ten time zones. I wake when I should sleep, and sleep when I should wake. Seek-ing the light out of doors, I walk, and everywhere, it is the doors that I see. According to Aldous Huxley, between things known and things unknown are the doors of perception. Maybe mine will open on a story idea.

At number thirty-eight Leeson Street, beyond night-dark-ened St. Stephen's Green, a figure leans against a gap in the Georgian iron fence, watching a door below street level. By the stairs a sign proclaims, *Angels*. The sign appears at dusk and disappears by half past three in the morning. The low door limits access to a VIP lap-dancing club that also caters Stag Parties and Fetish Nights as outreach programs. I am female, and, unlike seventy percent of Ireland's population, over forty-five. My muse jerks her chin in the direction of my hotel.

Above that same sidewalk in the normal light of day, I see a few matronly women emerge through Georgian doors from the stolid face of brick that fronts the length of the block. These rich doors are the style favored on cards and post-ers—scarlet, gold, cobalt, and black—each topped by its unique half-moon window. With white cloth the women dust the glossy paint, and burnish brass knockers that hang like torcs askew on the necks of gods and lions. Business people, bureaucrats, dental patients, and college students enter and exit the classic doors all day. Nothing remains to suggest that *Angels* ever existed.

I continue to dwell on the idea of doors—the mystery of them—as our coach drives deeper into the ancient province of Munster. A few days before, nine of us had gathered at a classic pub to assess our neonatal story ideas with our mentors. Responding to a primal summons, I left the others in an upholstered nook backed by staid paneling and followed directions downstairs through a labyrinth of turnings to a door marked with dignified lettering, *Toilet*. I stepped across the threshold into a different dimension, having had no more warning than a traveler who unwittingly enters the Otherworld by treading inside a toadstool ring.

Dim light fell on my vision, an eerie veil, concealing more than it revealed. Shapes emerged distorted by a black light that made the roll of tissue and the reflection of my teeth in its shiny holder a scalding white. The fluorescing vortex was more than I could bear. I fled to the narrow passage. Though I closed that door behind me, a surreal sense of dislocation pursued me up the stairs. My sharp sigh told me that I was glad I went, but no less glad to return to the ordinary world where everyone seemed to be the same age as when I left.

Today, our coach is rolling through what our local hostess, Sila, calls *The Rich Land*. It is verdant, fertile, and prosperous, the brightest facet on the Emerald Isle. She tells us the Irish love their land: the trees, the waters, the dark earth, the sacred winds and the hollow hills. History tells us that rain and rich land on this remote island, together with ancient Celtic tradition, germinated a culture of writers and poets; generations of storytellers, who, like shamans, pass through secret doors into the Otherworld and return to share its mysteries. Their stories have power to protect and heal. Still alive in modern Ireland is the belief that hearing certain stories on certain days can protect listeners from harm for a year.

When we reach Tipperary, we prowl the Rock of Cashel, an imposing limestone outcrop topped with three Gothic ruins. The original 11th century round tower points its finger at grey, indifferent heavens. Shattered by lightning and war, the thick stone walls of the 13th century cathedral rise in pocked arches, supporting no roof but the sky. Doors to piety, grandeur and intrigue, often defended by blood, are now gaping holes through which only the wind and the crows come and go. Kings and clerics, like the faery *Gentry*, have left the building, perhaps to return at Samhain with robes and teeth disquietingly white in atmospheres of altered light.

I feel haunted until I slip inside the small, 12th century chapel of King Cormac, pressed between the older tower and the younger cathedral, snug under its Romanesque ceiling. After the guide exits, I linger beside Cormac's empty and broken sarcophagus with its severed symbol of eternity. Coloratura Soprano, Debra Lynn, like some magical muse, offers a spontaneous *Ave Maria* to the spirit lingering in the sandstone arches and fresco fragments. Her entrancing voice and the answering cascade of harmonics transcend all time and space. The chapel and my heart throb with gratitude. I emerge in sunlight, but I do not return to ordinary consciousness until our coach crosses River Shannon into County Limerick. I am reminded that every door is both exit and entrance. My exit from the King's Chapel opened on a personal inscape seldom traveled, and Debra's soulful voice lingers on that threshold like cooled breath.

The next morning I set out alone, once more in search of story. I do not know as I descend the hill from Adare Manor through a mist of rain that I am about to find the key to all the doors I have seen in Ireland.

The old village rests on the site of 13th century *Ath Dara*, Ford of the Oak. Plaster walls and thatch roof frame the rough-hewn doors. Nostalgic of the Middle Ages, these quaint buildings were erected in 1820 to house the staff of the manor outside the gates, pretty replicas for the master's masquerade. A garish Kodak sign plugged into a medieval garden jolts me and turns me elsewhere on my quest. My fantasy does not include a Kodak moment; I wish to look into the true realm of magic and see magic looking back.

Then, I come upon the cat. Yawning and sitting bolt upright on her sill, she resembles the gargoyle on the east end of Dublin's Christchurch Cathedral, except for the wings. Her sharp glance yields no secrets. In fact, as I approach, she drops to the sidewalk and ghosts around the corner into a side street. Eager to be led anywhere, I follow.

The pavement extends ahead, vacant, and gray as twilight. The cat may as well have stepped on a *stray sod,* as one used to say of those who disappeared into the overlaying world of faery. Discouraged, I cross to the other side where a stone wall divides the grounds of the Trinitarian Abbey from the world beyond. The rain has ceased, but the light remains ambivalent. Low on optimism, I do not remove my hooded raincoat.

Two recessed crimson doors smolder in the side of the Abbey. I lean against the wet wall, which is chest high, to steady the camera. I zoom in on the branching iron bands that bind the door planks together, thinking of the heat of the forge, the smell of the sweat, and the sound of the hammers that formed them. But, I sense these doors are sealed, with silence and empty pews crowding the interior behind them. Further down the wall, I look over into the yard behind the Abbey. I raise the camera, lean toward the building, and focus on the shadowed form of a third door. It opens in the viewfinder.

Little girls in blue uniforms emerge, guided by four elders twice their size: a class of twenty-seven from Our Lady's Abbey Primary School. They file in an orderly procession toward neat bean rows in their garden—except one child who stands still as a stone in a stream, staring directly at me. All she could see above the wall would be a hood, one silver eye, and one hand: a Fomorian—primeval occupant of Ireland, a god of chaos—rearing its misshapen head to peer at her from the Otherworld.

Disconcerted by her steady gaze I walk on, moving away

as I go, so that the wall rises higher between us. At the end of it a round building with a slated dome completes the corner. Unlike the mortared wall, the stone block cylinder is smooth and worn, as if by hands. There is no visible door. Lichen dusts the surface with gold. Heavy foliage disallows the sight of the Abbey yard. The street I came down has no outlet, so I must go back the way I have come. I have no wish to be taken for the monster I am not, or the American tourist that I am, but when I reach the place I had stood, I cannot resist the urge to look across the wall again.

The elders are leading the children back indoors. While the others pass unaware across the threshold, the somber child holds my gaze, as if she had never stopped seeing me since that first glimpse. The girl, though facing a monster, is unafraid; and I, seeing the girl's courage, recognize the young, inexperienced mage from the novel I am writing back home. This time when I look into the realm of magic, magic is looking back. The blue-clad girl disappears from view, and the honey-colored door closes; but my mind still sees her watching me, with the eyes of my character, from the other side.

I wonder if, by creating and entering my characters, I am a shapeshifter. I become other beings, speak in other voices, and travel in different times to different worlds. So, I reason, I am a shaman, gaining and giving insight through eyes of heroes and antagonists. In the form of my heroine, I step through the gaps in everyday things where only the imagination can go, the doors of perception. Between the words, between the rules, is a world of danger and beauty that can break into ordinary consciousness.

At the interface, anything is possible, but as Initiate, I must learn how to enter and exit. Our mentors, all accomplished authors, show us the margin between unlike things, the point of contact between conflicting forces, and strange, grey areas that can go either way. From there we can follow our dread, our passion—or the cat—and enter the visionary state.

At this point in my thinking, it occurs to me that the doors of perception open both ways. Like *the Gentry, the Seelie Court,* or *the Good Folk* of Irish lore, our muses want to interact with us, as if they share our journey and hope to help and be helped along the way. Our muses, and the master storytellers challenging us in Ireland, lead us out of doors into the orderly bean rows and ask us to read between the lines.

Storytellers relive the unending tension between the darkness and the light, and reenact the perpetual clash of good and evil. This echoes the war in Eire between the primeval Fomorians and the civilized Children of Dana; a war that neither mythological force must win absolutely and forever. If one side won, what would become of our stories? And, we must have the stories.

Whether we are writers or readers, bards or listeners, we are eager to welcome storytellers returning from their journeys. We gather in the light of their fires. We enter the world of the tales and are drawn together by universal truths that inspire and sustain us. Our participation completes the magic. We exit, changed, into new spaces. More doors.

All my Irish doors begin to creak and bang, unhinged in the wind of memory. My mind opens to the belief that what stands between humanity and chaos is the power of story. As writers, poets, playwrights, or filmmakers, we recreate myth, give form to the unknowable, and make peace with life's ambiguities. We even learn to embrace the night. In our darker tales, we invite chaos into the firelight where it may be conquered, at least for a while.

In 1972, my stepsister Tina and I went to Ireland and rented a horse-drawn Gypsy caravan. We camped in farmers' fields and cooked over campfires. Sometimes we were invited in for a home-cooked meal, and got to listen to Irish stories, often told in song. It was one of the most amazing journeys of my life, and I've always been grateful to Tina that she talked me into it. She died of a stroke too young, almost three years ago. I miss her still, always will. So, this one's for you, Tina.

OUT OF TIME
by Judith G. Lyeth

July, 1972

My life simply didn't matter to me anymore. When my sister called out for me to come look at a tree, I really couldn't have cared less. But rather than give Karen more reason to worry over my depressed state of mind, I clambered to my feet and limped to the door of the Gypsy caravan replica. The unrelenting verdancy of the Irish countryside awaited me out there, and I sighed. All that burgeoning fertility, mocking me. Or so it seemed.

Karen reached out a hand to help me down the steep steps. "Alyssa? How're you doing?" she asked.

"All right," I replied, blinking in the sunlight that danced all over a landscape of green, cut only by grey dry stone walls, puffs of white sheep, and a muddy river. My shorter leg in its brace was throbbing more viciously than usual, but I didn't see the point of saying so.

I wondered again at our mother, who had practically forced this journey upon us. Yes, I'd always been enamored of Gypsies; I'd dressed as one for Halloween until I outgrew trick-or-treating and began reading about them instead. But this was insane. I was twenty-three, and had long ago put away childish dreams. But, thanks to an article in National Geographic about a new travel company in Ireland which was recreating the whole 'Gypsy Experience', Mom had shipped us here, to County Cork. For the next week, we'd be living just like the Gypsies did a couple hundred years ago: traveling and sleeping in a wildly painted wooden wagon, camping in farmers' fields at night, and being responsible for a large white horse with feathered feet. Karen had to do most of the work, which only made me feel more useless.

This trip to 'lift my spirits' after Peter broke our engagement wasn't working.

Guilt flooded me again, quickly followed by despair, over the pain I knew I was about to cause my family. I planned to end my life before this trip was done. I had a stash of Percodan. It was prescribed to ease my twisted leg but I didn't use them for that. As soon as I could design a way to escape my sister for a few hours, I would find a place to hide and take them all.

My heart would stop and I'd be free of the unrelenting pain. In my leg. In my heart.

My spirit was already dead, and I longed to follow.

"You don't have to be so brave, Lys," Karen said gently. "I saw you wince, I know when it hurts. But look." She pointed toward the river that bisected the farmer's field. "Did you ever see such an amazing tree?" Her angular face was alight with wonder. "Are you up for a peek underneath? It reminds of the weeping willow we used to have in the front yard."

I nodded. My sister could never resist trees; she often joked that she might have been a Druid in another life. And, I had to admit, this one did command attention. At least four stories high, it looked like a muscular cousin to a weeping willow, with bushy foliage and serrated round leaves. When we ducked through the drooping branches, I felt I'd entered the hush of a deep green cathedral. And it wasn't one tree, but three, growing side by side along the riverbank.

"Wow," Karen whispered, reaching out to touch the rough bark.

I agreed. I limped along the path that curved around the third trunk, drawn by the air of mystery in these green depths. As I went by the middle tree, I felt a curious ripple pass through my body and faint lights flickered at the edge of my sight. When I came out into the open once more, I could only stare in stunned surprise.

Before me lay a Gypsy camp, with a dozen caravans just like our replica, parked in a large circle. Same boxy shape, same bright colors and gaily painted designs. A great many voices spoke at once, and loudly, but I couldn't understand a word. Several horses were fenced together at one end of the field; the tang of hay and manure and wood smoke from several cooking fires scented the air. And the people were dressed as I'd done for my favorite holiday until I was ten. These days, I knew that Gypsies traveled in motor homes and dressed in modern clothes. Was this some kind of medieval re-creation? But, if that were true, we'd have heard this racket from the other side of the trees . . . wouldn't we?

I turned to ask my sister, but she was nowhere in sight.

I spun on my good leg, calling, "Karen! Come on! You've got to see this!" But she didn't emerge from the green tunnel. I sighed, not overly worried. She was most likely still communing with one of the trees and would catch up when she realized I'd moved on.

So I turned back to the Gypsy camp, wondering if I'd stumbled into a Renaissance Faire, Irish style. But as I watched, it soon became obvious that something was badly wrong. People milled about furiously, women either weeping or looking resolute, men pounding fists into their palms, cursing, and children either looking bewildered or crying.

A tiny, sloe-eyed girl caught sight of me, screamed, and pointed.

The camp fell silent and my neck prickled as approximately forty people turned to look. Two burly men, scowling fiercely, rushed over to me. The taller one sputtered something completely unintelligible.

I'd studied Gypsies; I knew they tended to be suspicious of strangers and treat them accordingly. "I'm sorry," I said, as politely as I could. "Do you speak English?"

The man spat. "Who you are? What you want?"

"I've just come through those trees behind me," I replied,

gesturing over my shoulder.

The man's swarthy face paled. Without another word, I was muscled to an empty wagon and flung inside. I landed hard on my bad leg; tears of agony sprang to my eyes and I knuckled them away. Then I heard something heavy drop and knew I was locked in.

My head spun; what the hell had just happened? It would seem I'd landed in a different time and space, but that was completely impossible. I shrugged, rubbing my leg. Hadn't we just rented a horse-drawn Gypsy caravan in this summer of 1972 that looked like it belonged in another century? There had to be a logical explanation.

If not a Renaissance Faire, perhaps this was a movie set, and I'd ruined a shot.

I heard a scraping sound. The door clicked, and creaked open. An old woman, dressed in voluminous black skirts and a shawl, stood in the doorway, leaning on a cane. She looked down at me, sprawled on the floor. I sat up and stared back, at black eyes in a massively wrinkled face, surrounded by a corona of straggly grey hair. To my surprise, I saw no hostility in that gaze; instead, I caught a gleam of excitement in those exotic, ancient eyes.

The old one raked her gaze over me, reaching out her cane to lift the hem of my jeans. "Woman dressed as man, *mahi'mei*—forbidden, unclean," she said in thickly accented English. "Though I sensee hurt." She squatted down and rolled up the denim, revealing my shrunken calf. A livid bruise was already forming above the ugly metal brace. "What happen to leg?"

"I had polio as a baby," I replied. "A sickness that left me lame. But the bruise is from the fall, when your men tossed me in here. Will you tell me why I've been locked in?"

"First you tell," she said. "You come of nowhere. Who you? Where from?"

"I'm from America," I said. "I'm here with my sister. We rented a caravan just like this in Cork, which is now parked in Mr. O'Donnell's field, just beyond those trees."

"Where America?"

"You've never heard of America? The United States? Across the Atlantic ocean?" I couldn't believe it. I knew Gypsies were self-contained, but this was beyond belief.

To my surprise, the woman's face creased into a satisfied smile. "Ah-ha! You come across waters of Ocean?" At my nod, the crone chuckled and began muttering to herself, carrying on an internal conversation. At last she looked up at me with those intense black eyes and spoke aloud. "You come from *Other* place. *Other* time." She said it with decision.

A knot of fear formed in my belly. "What do you mean, 'other time'?"

"*Other* time, future," said the crone. "DreamSeer say other may come from future in time to help. You come through trees that hold timegate."

I remembered that odd tingle when I passed through the trees. The fear spread from my gut to encircle my heart. "What year is it now, for you?"

"*Gadgei* reckoning, year-lord 1679."

I went numb with shock. This had to be a bizarre dream that I would awaken from at any moment. "That's impossible!" I cried. "There's no such thing as time travel."

"Oh?" The woman's eyes twinkled. "You no believe in magic?"

"Of course not," I said, wishing I did.

"Too bad," she replied. "Magic believe in you."

I drew a long breath. *Play along,* I told myself. *Get her to talk to me.* "If what you say is true, what am I doing here?"

Knees creaking, the old one sat down, facing me. "First, give names, say greet words. Me, Gabrella. I greet you." She reached out a gnarled hand, palm facing outward.

I recognized the ritual from my studies. Barely touching my palm to hers, I responded, "I greet you in turn, Gabrella. My name is Alyssa."

"Good greet, Alyssa." She took a breath and began to speak. "Three nights since, men from village come. Accuse chief's son of stealing horse. Not true. Chief and son fight with them. Village men go. Next night, comes priest and more village men, to take Callinda. Our Healer. Call her witch.

Tonight's sunset, they say she burn. We no let her burn. We bring her back, then send through trees with you. Need one from other time to take her through. So. You come. So. We retrieve Callinda. Then, you take her. She go. She safe in *Other* time."

The old woman absolutely believed every word she spoke, and I found myself falling under the spell of her conviction. "But . . ." I bit my lip. "How can I take someone from the seventeenth century back into the twentieth? What will she do? Where will she go?"

"She find our people in your time. You no worry. You take her through timegate, she be fine, you go on with life."

And isn't that a grand irony? I thought dryly. I had no intention of going on with my life. If I really *had* stepped through some kind of time-warp, what better way to escape Karen and carry out my plan? The old lady said they needed me, to bring their Healer through the trees. Where was the harm in doing as she asked? Timegate or not, I could still die once I got her to the other side . . . Slip back under those green depths and swallow my pills . . .

"If you need my help, why am I locked in here?"

"Men no understand who, what you are. Angry that Callinda taken, angry we lose her either way. You stranger. Lock you up till they send for me. Sorry for hurt." She reached out a bony hand and placed it on my bruised calf. "You hurt deeper inside than this, though, no?"

I felt a warmth, almost a tingle, which eased the aching leg. "Are you a Healer, too?"

"No more. Passed power to Callinda, grand-daughter. Only have trace now. But, you help us, take Callinda through trees, she maybe can help you."

"Heal my leg?"

"Maybe heal pain of leg, if no lameness. How willing you, to let hurt go?"

Startled, I thought about that. I'd been in pain most of my life. Many were amazed I wasn't addicted to my medication, but I couldn't stand the thought of further dependency. Was I truly willing to let the pain go? I was willing to die to end it, but *let it go*? The obvious answer was 'yes', but something kept that word behind my teeth. Pain had defined my whole life; I couldn't imagine living without it. Quite frankly, I'd rather not be living at all.

"I . . . want to say 'totally'," I replied at last. "But I'm not sure that would be true."

"Good. You no lie to self. Pain in heart worse than pain in leg, yes?"

Tears welled up as I nodded. Peter, the love of my life since junior high, had broken our engagement when the doctors discovered I would never bear a child. His enormously wealthy and powerful father, Peter Biggs III, had never approved of me, because of my deformity. I simply wasn't good enough to be part of that family. His son held out for ten years, remaining steadfast and loyal. He'd been my best friend and champion in junior high; then, in the ninth grade, we fell in love. Went steady all through high school. Got engaged our sophomore year in college. The withered leg never bothered him; he'd always made me feel beautiful inside. But he badly wanted his own children, and my barrenness was the final straw for his father. The break-up left me feeling shattered. Worthless. Now, I simply wanted to be done. I was tired of being lame, a burden on my family, the object of well-intentioned and barely veiled pity.

I didn't have the energy to continue living a life I didn't want.

"Yes," I replied, wiping away the tears. "I don't know how you know that, but you're right."

Gabrella smiled, her eyes compassionate. "You help us, we help you. Maybe you find reasons to want it again."

I stared in shock. Was the woman reading my mind?

"Thoughts clear on face," Gabrella said softly.

I swallowed hard, unwilling to discuss this further. "What do I have to do?"

"Tonight, we retrieve Callinda from village. Then, quick, you go through trees, so villagers no can take her again. Other side, she try help you with pain."

"I don't know if that's possible," I said. "But I'm willing

to help if I can. Am I just supposed to leave her there, in O'Donnell's field?"

"O'Donnell family owns field now," Gabrella said. "Same as your time. Family know secret of trees, is long-time friend to our people. They help. Callinda find her own, you no worry for her after. Only take her through. Understand?"

Surreptitiously, I stroked the pocket in which I kept my pills. What did it matter if any of this was real? Perhaps the last act of my life—even as a fantasy or dream—could have some meaning after all, and then I could finally be done with it. "All right," I said.

"You agree?" Gabrella stood, spat in her palm and held out her hand.

I stifled the urge to draw back, and returned the gesture, knowing this was the Gypsy way of sealing a bargain. "I agree. It feels like the right thing to do."

"Good," said the old woman as our hands clasped. I felt that same tingling warmth when Gabrella's damp palm met mine as when she touched my leg. "Now, you come." She led me out of the caravan and over to a bench near the central fire pit. "You sit. You wait."

I watched as the crone approached a knot of men and began to speak. Tension throbbed in the air; every now and then, one of the men would dart a suspicious glance at me. Eventually, though, they seemed to accept what the ancient one said. One by one, they shrugged, nodded, and then slipped away, their movements already stealthy.

Gabrella returned to my side. "So," she said. "They go, help bring Callinda back."

"How will they rescue her?"

"Burning at sunfall," she replied. "We all do own part. Men distract, women work magic. Make up minds, choose, we will all do," she added confidently.

I hoped she was right. From what I knew of the so-called Burning Times in Europe during the 1600's, they would need magic, for rescue was well-nigh impossible. Somehow, I had begun to care about this strange old woman personally, and what happened to her grand-daughter. It had been so long since I'd cared about anything, the feeling surprised me.

As the light began to lower toward afternoon, the old lady told me what she called the true history of the Gypsies. It varied greatly from what I'd learned in school, but I didn't argue. If they wanted to believe that their ancestors escaped the third destruction of Atlantis and settled in Egypt before dispersing throughout Europe, I guessed it wouldn't matter to them that the linguists claimed they hailed from northern India. But the tales of magic and alchemy intrigued me, and I wanted to learn more.

And I found myself surprised to be thinking about something as though I had a future.

When the colors of sunset streaked across the sky, the women emerged from the caravans and built up the central fire. When it was blazing fiercely, Gabrella stood, motioning me to follow. "Is law of nature: like calls like," she said. "So. We use power of Elements. Villagers put Callinda in fire, so we use power of fire, bring her through flames, theirs to ours. Men make noise, distract." She smiled at my look of disbelief, and nodded. "You no understand, no matter. Still join circle. Then after, you take her, to your time."

I sighed, very much afraid this was a dream after all.

Gabrella shook her head. "Is no belief in magic for the *gadgei* in your time?"

"No," I replied, almost sadly, for all at once I wanted to believe, at least in the possibility of it. "Magic is for children and crazy people."

"Too bad. No matter. We believe, we do. Come." The old woman brought me into the circle around the fire; as one, the women began to chant. I felt power begin to build, it pressed on my skin, prickled behind my eyes. The fire grew higher and higher, and I saw all the colors of the rainbow dancing in the flames. The circle of women began to dance in time with the chanting, forming a spiral that built upon itself. Though I couldn't understand the words, I felt the power of their focused will, their intention. Between the sound and movement, energy built to the point where I thought my ears might explode.

The dance came to a stop; the women dropped their hands and flung them skyward. I had a vision of a vast cone shooting off into the evening, arcing through the sky. Time suspended, we all held our breath, waiting . . . waiting . . . Suddenly, there was a loud crackle of lightning, and a body tumbled forth from the flames.

A woman lay on the ground, moaning in pain. She was burnt black, her feet gone.

Gabrella turned pale and jabbered orders in her own tongue. She flung her cloak over the injured woman, murmuring incessantly. Women scurried about, collecting medicinal supplies.

I stared in dismay, tears trickling down my face. I doubted the woman could survive. And even if she did, how was I to get the poor lady through the time gate when she couldn't walk? I certainly couldn't carry her. I looked at the prone figure and shuddered. Though she was covered now, I'd never forget the excruciating sight of that burned, oozing, blackened flesh, the sound of the woman's agony.

Well, I had an answer to that, at least. I dug the pills out of my pocket and went to kneel beside the old woman. "Gabrella," I said, "I guess the *gadgei* do have magic after all." I showed her the foil packet. "This will take away her pain."

The crone looked at me, then at the packet in my hand. "Is so?"

I nodded. "Make her swallow these." I opened the foil and held forth two.

Picking up one of the Percodan tablets, Gabrella studied it minutely. "Is medicine for pain?" I nodded. "Is your medicine?" Again, I nodded. "And works for you?"

"It does. But she mustn't take too much at once."

Those dark eyes stared into mine, seeing what I'd endeavored to hide from my family. "And you no use anymore?"

I shook my head. I hadn't taken them for months, saving them for a darker purpose. Extra Strength Excedrin got me through most days, if just barely. "Will she live, Gabrella?"

Gabrella sighed. "No. Villagers start fire early, that why she burnt so bad. She hover now between worlds. She no come back to us. This . . . damage too much. But is gift to take away pain of passing . . ." She spoke to the woman beside her, who proffered a mortar and pestle. Another provided water; in short order the two Percodan tablets were rendered liquid and dribbled between the injured woman's lips. Relief came much faster than I expected; within minutes the glaze of pain receded in her dark eyes, which she turned on me.

"Come," she whispered between blistered lips. The damage to her face wasn't nearly as severe as to her lower body. I knelt by her side. "I thankee, milady," she said, sounding much more Irish than her grandmother. "Will ye let me gi' ye a gift in return?"

Touched, I shook my head. "No, that's not necessary, really. Save your strength, please. If we can get you back to my time, there are doctors, hospitals, treatments—"

Callinda looked at me steadily. "No *gadgei* medicine can heal this, milady, in this time or any other. I go now, to a place beyond damage and pain. But first, I would try to help ye as ye helped me." Fathomless, wise eyes, though not as ancient as Gabrella's, stared into mine.

"All right, then," I said, realizing this was important to her, a dying wish.

"Are ye sure?" I nodded. "Gi' me yer hand, then?"

I did so, and felt something pass from Callinda into me, flooding me with a sense I could only describe as well-being, contentment. My eyes widened and I drew in a breath. "What *was* that?"

"'Tis the healing balm, passed from me to ye, as my granny passed it to me," Callinda replied. "Use it as ye will, lass."

"What does that mean?" I cried. "What have you done?"

"She pass power to you," Gabrella explained. "She no can take with her."

"But why? Why me?" My heart thudded.

"Why not you?" Gabrella smiled.

"I'm not even a Gypsy! I'm going back . . ." my words trailed off. To what? To die?

"Ye might stay," Callinda whispered. "Live here. Use gift for Tribe. Up to ye. Goodbye, lass. Thank ye for the boon." Her next words were in the Gypsy language, to Gabrella. Then the murmurs ceased; I watched her draw a last quiet breath, and let go.

The women gathered in a circle and began to sing her soul into the next world.

The tears coursed down my face as my mind whirled with new possibilities.

Something had changed inside me. I felt better than I ever had, stronger. The persistent pain in my leg was all but gone, reduced to a manageable ache. I reached down to roll up my jeans; the nasty bruise was receding. I knew I'd always have a limp, nothing could fix that, but not fighting pain every moment of every day if I stayed here made life seem almost worth living.

I had been invited to stay, whatever that meant. And I wanted to.

OK then, why not? Why shouldn't I?

Karen was no doubt freaking out by now. I smiled wryly, imagining my sister questioning the poor farmer. If I stayed here, a full-out search would ensue, bringing no end of trouble to the O'Donnells. I hadn't planned to return from this trip in any event, but with my suicide, at least the family would have a body and a letter, an answer to what had happened. Could I simply disappear without a word, leaving them with such an unsolved mystery?

No. I'd have to go back and try to explain this to Karen.

My sister was more inclined to believe in magic than I. Could I convince her? If so, wouldn't it be easier on the family to imagine I'd gone off to another place—one where I could be happy—rather than deal with a dead body and suicide note? I'd discovered in the past hour that my life did matter after all, but not the life I'd left behind.

The thought of going back pressed on me, made it hard to breathe.

Thoughts of being free from the pitying looks, of no longer feeling lame and useless, of never seeing Peter or his father again, of the freedom to be someone new, made me want to sing.

If—no, *when* I didn't return, Mom and Dad would be distraught. Would their pain be any less if they knew for sure I was dead? Or, would it help if they had the possibility of magic to cling to in their grieving, and that I'd found some for myself?

I wasn't going home in any case.

I looked up, into Gabrella's black eyes. "So," the crone said. "You will stay?"

"Why would you want me to? I'm *gadgei*. Wouldn't that be a problem?"

"No problem. Tribe see Callinda pass power to you. Now, Tribe need you. Healer."

"How can I possibly be a Healer? I have no training!"

Gabrella smiled. "Knowledge inside you, now. I teach, you learn. You will stay?"

The tribe needed me. The idea that I could actually be useful and live a productive life, free of the constant pain, lifted my heart and I felt happy, hopeful, for the first time in far too long. And there I had my answer. I had a right to live a life of my own choosing, didn't I?

"First, I must go back, tell my sister what I'm doing, but yes. I would very much like to stay." Karen would want to tie me up and ship me home in a box, but I had to try to make her understand.

Gabrella shook her head. "Magic always has price," she said. "Is in balance now."

"So, if I go back, I can't return?"

"Not without new price. Magic demands its own."

I decided I didn't need to know what that meant, just yet, anyway. If the price was a life, I didn't *want* to know. "Can someone get word to my family?"

"Where is family?"

"My sister is in O'Donnell's field, with a caravan and a white horse, no doubt raising hell with the poor man about where I've gone. My parents are in America."

Gabrella's face creased into a smile. "O'Donnell explain to sister. Sister explain to mother and father."

"But . . . will she believe him?" Karen just might, in time; I needed to believe that she would before I could agree to stay. And I badly wanted to stay.

The old woman winked. "He *Irishman,* like one who teach Callinda speak your words. Has silver blarney-tongue. Make *anyone* believe *anything!*"

And there it was, what I needed.

I laughed a little, knowing she spoke true, even though I'd only been in Ireland for three days. "Forgive me, Karen," I whispered, "and I love you, Mom and Dad. But now, here, I finally have a chance to live a life that matters, and I need to take it. I'm going to grab it for all I'm worth. Be glad for me."

There was a young writer from Maui,
Who believed that his prose would quite wow me.
But I set him straight,
Said "Your prose ain't so great,
So his publishing dreams went Kapowee!

—Terry Brooks

Just prior to my trip to Ireland to attend the Maui Writer's Retreat, I had asked my Aunt Suzie, our family historian, for information of my Irish heritage. □ She sent this letterwhich had been found in some of my family's memorabilia. □ It was written to my great grandmother Maggie McShea Keenan, who was living in America, from her cousin Honora, in Ireland. □ This is a real slice of Irish life in 1939 and gives a colorful impression of the political and social landscape. □ It is simple, direct and full of Irish charm. □

A Letter from Honora
contributed by Jerry Eiting

Queenstown, Ireland
December 21, 1939

Dear Cousin:

Your welcome letter was received and me and Aunt Bridget thank you kindly for the money you sent. We had seven masses said for your grandfather and grandmother. God rest their souls.

You have gone high places in America, God bless you. I hope you have not forsaken your native land.

Your cousin, Hughie Doherty, was hung in Londonderry last Friday for killing a policeman. May God rest his soul, and may God's curse be on Jimmy Rodgers, the informer. May his soul burn in hell. God forgive me.

Times are not as bad as they might be. The herring is back and everyone, or nearly everyone, has a boat or an interest in one and the price of fish is good, thanks be to God.

The Orangemen are terrible. They go through the country in their lorries and shoot the poor people down in the fields where they are working. God's curse on them.

Your Uncle Denny took a shot at one of them yesterday from the hedge, but he had too much to drink and missed him. God's curse on the drink.

Well, I hope this letter finds you and your family well and happy, and we all join in sending our best wishes. May God bless you all. Am sorry you're not with us.

The Dohertys are a hundred strong men since the best of them have stopped going to America. They will cover the whole countryside.

Father O'Flaherty, who baptized your distant cousin, and who is now feebleminded, sends his blessing.

May God rest you and yours and keep you from sickness and sudden death.

Your Cousin,
Honora

P.S. Things are not quite as bad as they seem. Every police barrack and every Protestant church in the country has been burned down. Thanks be to God.

After twenty years of working and visiting Ireland I discovered St Patrick's Cathedral was Anglican. I obviously had never asked or discussed it before, assuming that it was Catholic. The literature and guides talked about St Patrick as if he were part of the Anglican heritage. Hard to take for an American raised in the Roman Catholic tradition.

IT AIN'T RIGHT

by Mike Malaghan

Dempsey, one of the two panhandlers, sat, his seedy brown-trousered legs spread out in front him. His back rested against the corrugated bark of an oak tree planted the year before the Easter uprising. The lush, closely-woven grass soothed his bottom like a cushion. Nature's perfume from adjacent row of rose bushes in St. Patrick's Park roused his senses. He looked up at Dublin's spired and naved granite Cathedral of the same name just as the sun slipped behind its tower.

Both beggars wore the uniform of their trade, as though they had been fastidious in choosing just the right haberdashery. In fact, they had. Their brown shoes had been picked from the finest trash bins next to the Trinity College student housing area. Each wore one shoe without a lace, although they kept the missing lace in their blue denim jackets and reinserted it when their coin collecting had finished. Their costumes were topped off by caps from the 1940s, which they had stumbled upon outside a theater putting on a Beckett play.

The liver blotches they sported were genuine enough and rightly earned, the steady inflow of stout giving their forty-something-old bodies that sixty-year-old look.

They groomed their long snowy beards daily. The two would have made a Harvard marketing grad proud the way they had, side-by-side, tested combed and trimmed beards versus unkempt and snagged. More would-be-folks-of-charity blithely passed by nasty and snarled facial hair, while occasionally favoring the neater look, by dropping a coin into their Kellogg's single serving cereal container, chosen for its subliminal suggestion that each offering went toward healthy sustenance.

The frayed look of their church-given brown trousers added another authentic touch. The two panhandlers had spent the better part of an evening rubbing the cuffs on a curbside. A clothesline rope made do as a belt to crimp the oversized waistbands emphasizing that smart emaciated look. They still bathed to increase coinage, but not as often as they used to.

A pathetic lot. And right proud of it.

"It ain't right, you know," said Dempsey, staring at the front tower of the grey marble cathedral.

"What's that?" asked Lanahan, who had not been paying attention, concentrating instead on counting his change from the morning shift. If you got a corner on Paddy's park on a sunny day, the pickings were good.

"I'm saying, you dense lout, it ain't right. St. Patrick's Cathedral being run by the prods."

"Ah, that again. Quit harping on old history. They'd be paying for it. Five centuries, more or less. And when it fell into ruin, the Guinness folks built it again."

"You never get it, do ya, Lanahan. The bloody Brits weren't just happy enough to steal our land, our language, and then starving half of us to death. They stole St. Patrick, our very own patron saint. This being the very church good Catholics built on the exact spot Paddy did his baptisms. Then, a thousand years later, Henry the Eighth stole it in-between murdering his wives. It ain't right, I'm telling ya."

"Ah, Jesus, Mary, and Joseph, will you look up and see what's coming our way."

Two burly police marched in their direction with a mean purpose.

"Ah, fucking sod all. And we be having such a good day of it," said Dempsey.

The taller of the two blue-uniformed young men ordered,

"Off, you two. How many times do you have to be warned? We should be taking you over to the station. And would too, if wasn't such a fine day—too fine to waste on the sorry likes of you. Now, git over to the Temple Bar where you belong."

In character, Dempsey and Lanahan began their shuffle over to the quay. In the early years, when their panhandling hours were finished and they left their working area, they would resume walking in a normal gait. Some evenings they would even change into regular clothes and return to their panhandling area to eat in a decent pub as normal people, having a hoot at the incongruity of it.

Now the sad characters they created had morphed into reality.

Last week Dempsey had spotted blood in his stool. Yesterday the nuns at the charity hospital said he had spots on a hardening liver. The good Sister Mary Margaret had told him, "Your liver's crusting like the edge of burnt toast, so brittle you could snap pieces off with your pinkie. It's the disappearing spongy part of what's left of your liver that must process all your poison. If you don't stop your liquid ways, you will be peeing blood all too soon." And sure enough, this very morning, his stream was as a pink as a blushing colleen on her wedding night.

He hadn't told Lanahan. He'd find out soon enough. The countdown had begun, and he not even being fifty. He'd seen the end-game wards at Sisters of Mercy Hospital. Twelve to a room. And they checking who's breathing each morning.

He resumed the mantra. "It ain't right. We should do something about it."

"Leave it alone, Dempsey. Let's just get a Guinness and enjoy the glory of the day."

Dempsey walked along, sullen. He would have bursts of mental energy—true, more infrequently now—that could last as long as a day. It was then he'd recall his being a student at Trinity before being thrown out over a silly incident of a bar fight—well, maybe more than one, truth be told. Many had done far worse and got off with a reprimand. Occasionally, and only at night, he would piss on the side of one of the walls of the college to remind the snooty know-it-alls that he hadn't forgotten the injustice.

Lanahan kept quiet when Dempsey fell into these moods. He worried not a bit about his own lot in life. He'd been brought up dirt poor. Never knew his father, who had left his mum when Lanahan had been but a wee one, to take up with another woman. Divorce wasn't allowed in those days, but it hadn't kept his mum from finding companionship. Sometimes a bloke would stay for six months. Most never beat him.

"Another one," grumbled Dempsey, looking at Christ Church, former Catholic, now Anglican, at the intersection of the street that bore the same name as the church and Werburgh.

To the immediate right sat the Bull & Castle Pub. It was off-limits to them. Pub by pub they managed to wear out their welcome with their Guinness-induced donnybrooks. Across the street they looked at Puck's Alley, a pub they had left on their own a year ago before being asked to leave. It would be safe to return. But not today. They would hold it in reserve.

They hadn't spoken about where they were going; it wasn't necessary. Like a dog coming home, they ambled right, left, and straight as they had for most of two decades. Their feet knew the shortest distance to Turk's Head at Parliament and Essex from any location. It was the one pub were an occasional donnybrook—low-level, mind you, and between friends—wouldn't make it impossible to return.

The bartender looked up as the two ne'er-do-wells walked in, wrinkling his nose in recognition. Turk's Head was a serious drinking bar frequented by all classes if they didn't mind boisterous debate, crude sexist remarks, and the tangy sweat of men who made an honest living. Dempsey and Lanahan came as close to fitting in with the eclectic lot in this pub as any they could find.

Like the churches the two bums had passed, the bar had little naves for those small groups who wanted to pray with their pints in relative privacy. At this mid-afternoon hour, only a small contingent of all-day drinkers had settled in.

"We got cash, laddie. Don't you worry none. How about two pints of Guinness, the foreign one, not that weak stuff," referring to strongest of the three Guinness choices. This was one of the few bars who offered the heftier brew more popular in Africa and Asia.

"Look at 'im, Dempsey. A fucking Pole serving bar in a proper Irish pub. It's hard to find a pub who hires one of our own. And we needing the jobs."

"That's what I'm saying, Lanahan. The country's going down the shitter. And we ain't doing nothing about it. It's late in the day for us. What we ever done that's important?"

"I don't want to do anything important. I just want a Guinness and have a few quid to pay the rent. We got a good life, we do. The pickings have been good the last few years. Folks got change in their pockets nowadays."

"That's your problem, Lanahan. You never wanted to be anybody. I do. I could've been, you know."

"You're always dreaming about could've and should've. Me? I'm satisfied. And look at ya, will ya. You be the same as me, but I'm the more happy about it."

"Think about that church, Lanahan. Our St. Patrick church run by Anglicans with lady vicars. It's an abomination. We could do something about it, we could."

"You're always complaining about some big issue. You ranted and raved about giving up our Irish currency, shouted and pouted about changing the divorce law. On and on you go. And me a punchboard for it all. And you doing nothing."

"I would do something if I had a partner who was willing and not so pleased being a nobody, going nowhere, doing nothing."

Lanahan got up, went to the bar, and brought back two more Guinness. He had his retort ready.

"Oh, look at ya. Always the big talker. Blaming Trinity College for your bad-tempered ways, the government, me, or anyone for your lost dreams. All we is, is panhandlers. And good ones. We even have a flat, not big enough to swing a cat, but still not sleeping in the streets. No taxes. If we get really sick, the hospitals have got to take us in."

"Lanahan, think of them Moslem boys who blew up the tube in London. They saw injustice against them and acted like the lads in the IRA."

"What nonsense you be talking. They're heathens killing innocents."

"Maybe so. But did you hear the bobbies in London are getting extra training to be more sensitive to the Pakis? The councils are starting more programs for them. The bombers won, for God's sake. They got respect."

"Your problem, Dempsey, is watching the telly all the time and them news channels. Give it up. Don't matter none." He paused to belch and said, "We come, we live, we die."

"And do ya think there would have been a peace settlement in the North with all the new rights for the Catholics if the IRA hadn't bombed the prods for years?"

"It's your turn to get the Guinness."

The waiter greeted Dempsey with a surly look.

"You're getting a bit loud. You need to be quiet or you will have to drink elsewhere."

"Sure, mate. And where you come from, everyone drinks in silence now, don't they." Dempsey waited for his fifty pence change, making sure not to leave a tip. He always had a reason.

Placing the Guinness on the ancient cherry wood table, Dempsey renewed his barrage.

"After Independence, we should have taken the church. You wouldn't think of letting the Brits keep the post office or custom houses, would ya? You know if Michael Collins had lived, he would have taken over the church. He would have."

"You be talking nonsense. Besides, it was one of our own bullets that found the back of Mick. Sometimes we be better at killing our own than the bloody Brits."

"No, it is you who's talking cowardly nonsense. All your life you wanted to be nobody and brag about it. I could be somebody. Strike a blow for Ireland."

"Then go do it, for bloody sake, and get off my arse."

"You see, you always be knocking me down. It's you who should appreciate me. You were a bum. I showed you how to become a panhandler. You think you'd be living in a flat without me?"

"Right you are, but what's that got to do with St. Paddy's? Let me get a more couple pints."

"In a minute. You know, Lanahan, we're getting along in years. You know the hospital told us about our livers and all. The days we got ain't as many as before. I don't want to be stacked in a pauper's grave and have to tell St. Pete I never done nothing in me whole life."

His hand tightened around the neck of his Guinness. He started to lift it, then remembered it was empty. Lanahan kept his eyes down. The tenor on the sound system crooned, *"Oh Danny Boy, the pipes, the pipes, are calling."* They paused to listen. Were there tears in their eyes when the song reached the mid-point?

When and if you come, when all the flowers are dying
And I am dead, as dead I well may be

Dempsey thought of his pink stream into the bowl that very morning. He couldn't listen anymore.

"Look up, Lanahan. We still got a chance, you and I, to be somebody, to strike a blow for Ireland before it's too late for us."

"Rubbish. I don't want to hear about your death talk again. You're always talking about dying. Go die, for God's sake, and leave me to living."

"We can wrap ourselves in dynamite and go into St. Patrick's. They never check you. Just pay the entrance fee and walk in big as life. We could march right to the main altar."

"Mary, mother of Christ, you talking suicide, you being a Catholic and all. Committing suicide in a church. And where you be getting dynamite, me laddie? You're gonna call Jerry Adams and tell him you're ready to start it all over again? You're daft."

"It'd be like a crusader. They knew they'd die, but they died for a reason. Just once, Lanahan, we could be somebody. Somebody who everyone remembered like Collins, Parnell, O'Connor."

"I'm sick of your talk. Big talk. Never doing nothing. Always blaming me for you being nothing but a drunk begging for his pennies every day. You're nothing. You're going die nothing. And if I die before you, no one will even know you're dead."

Two college-looking youngsters walked in. Dempsey glanced at them. Slumming for a day, he thought. He remembered his wild days at Trinity in places like this. He could hear the provost again, as he had so many times.

"Dempsey, you have run out of chances. The last warning was exactly that. You have to pack up and leave by six this evening."

Why hadn't he enrolled in another college instead of letting his uncle talk him into working with him at the docks? "Just for a while, mind you," he'd said. Dempsey could have been a teacher. And a good one too.

The two students sat down at the bar. Dempsey's attention returned to Lanahan, trying to regain the thread of thought. He had something important to say today. He had.

"I am somebody. I could be somebody. You is the nothing. Nothing for yourself. Nothing for me. Holding me back all these years. Now we have a chance to get St. Paddy's back and you won't lift a fucking finger."

"'Lift a finger,' he says. What have you ever done except get enough coins so we could eat for a single day? And many a day not even that. You're a coward whipping me with your words because you spent more time in school and can read books. I'm your friend because you can feel superior to me. You're a nobody, always will be."

Dempsey swept the Guinness off the table with his right hand. Then he put both hands under the table to tip it over.

"No you don't," barked Lanahan in a stupor, but still quick enough to respond at the attempt to turn the table into him. "Have a bit of your own." He drove the table back before Dempsey could lift more than a few inches, knocking him down on the floor spread eagled next to the red brick wall.

Dempsey let out a yelp as his tailbone landed smartly, firing piercing needle points from spine to skull and back again.

The bartender rushed from behind the counter to stop the fray.

Dempsey snatched a rolling bottle of Guinness by its neck.

Lanahan taunted, "Now see what you done. Who will take us now?"

The maddening pain incited a new fury in Dempsey, breaking through the alcoholic indolence. Lanahan stood over him. He felt the adrenaline kick in.

Still on the floor, Dempsey swung the bottle into the brick wall, cracking it hard, breaking off the bottom. He rose from the floor, eyes glaring at Lanahan, shaking the black jagged glass like a wild-eyed school marm making a point at the front of the class.

"Our chance to give back to Ireland what's ours and you spit on it."

Dempsey sensed, but ignored the gathering crowd.

The bartender shouted, "Out, you two!" But, seeing the jagged weapon, kept his distance. Dempsey turned toward the intrusion.

Lanahan brought him back. "The man's right, you know. Let's go."

If not for the spinal pain, if not for the regret of a wasted life, if not for the sense that life's clock stood close to midnight, that might have been the end of it. Instead, Dempsey jerked the bottle in a frenzy, punctuating his rage,

"Are you going to St. Paddy's with me or not?"

Lanahan step forward to disarm his friend. "Forget St. Paddy for the day."

"No! No more tomorrows. Are you coming with me or not?" he shouted, still shaking his fist, extended by the broken Guinness bottle.

Lanahan started to move forward, lifting his leg to make the step. He came down on one of the strewn bottles, slipped and fell forward into the jerking point of Dempsey's unintentional scalpel. The razor-edged Guinness dagger sliced Lanahan's carotid artery.

Blood spouted.

Lanahan grabbed his surging throat.

He continued to fall forward.

The spewing blood splashed Dempsey's face. He reached out to grab his falling companion. Both fell to the ground, the blood still rocketing.

Lanahan looked up at his crimson fountain of life, held Dempsey tight, and gurgled, "It ain't right."

Pigeons and Crumbs was inspired by a combination of the at-mosphere of St. Stephen's Green and a song called "Dublin Sky," by Darren Hayes. While the lyrics of the song are nothing like the story, it is the tone and the feeling of the music that inspired the main character's mood and back story. From there I had a jumping point, and the pigeons helped me come up with the rest.

PIGEONS AND CRUMBS

by Aimée Carter

"Mind if I sit here?"

Frowning, Daniel looked up from staring out across the pond on the opposite side of the walkway, instead focusing on the person who'd interrupted the mournful silence. Stand-ing next to the bench on which he sat was a redheaded pixie who looked to be no more than twenty-three, and she didn't wait for his answer before she plopped down heavily next to him. Daniel automatically scooted down the bench, mov-ing as far away from her as he could.

On his walk from the cemetery to the park, Daniel had promised himself over and over again that he wouldn't cry. He couldn't cry, not yet, because crying meant that she was really dead, and he wasn't ready to accept that. His fingers curled around the metal armrest of the bench as he consid-ered standing. He'd waited all day to be here, to have a few moments of peace and quiet to miss his wife. Now that this inconsiderate girl had robbed him of his time alone, he won-dered if it was even worth it to remain in such a painful place, the place where he'd proposed. Releasing the bar to twist his wedding band around his ring finger, he glanced nervously at the girl, unsure of how to react, when he noticed the silent tears streaming down her cheeks.

Just as he was about to stand, her shaky voice whispered through the air, freezing him in place. "You're too bloody young to be feeding the pigeons, you know."

Daniel stared at her indignantly, as if she'd just purposely insulted the memory of his wife. Less than ten feet away from where he sat was a stone bridge, where he'd met Miranda nearly twenty years ago, as they both fed the pigeons. He'd run out of bread and she'd offered him some of hers, and it was then that their relationship started. It was one of those moments that he needed to remember, needed to feel again as he drifted inside a fog of fiercely suppressed pain and loss.

"I'm not feeding the pigeons."

"Then why are they crowding around you?" the girl said, meeting the challenging look he gave her with a tearful gaze. Unable to give her any sort of answer that he thought satisfactory, he merely shrugged and looked down at his hands, examining the intricate Celtic carvings on his wedding band. Miranda had picked it out, insisting he had no taste when it came to that sort of thing. He'd readily agreed.

After a brief silence, she spoke again, this time in a much friendlier voice with all traces of her earlier anguish gone. "I'm Tori. Sorry if we disturbed you earlier."

Glancing at her out of the corner of his eye, he conceded that she wasn't going to stop staring until he answered her. In that moment he took a closer look and recognized her as part of the couple who'd been wreaking havoc in the park as he'd walked in. He'd mostly ignored the fight, too lost in his grief to pay much attention to anything, but he'd been aware of it. "Daniel, and you didn't."

"Liar." Her catty grin offended him more than her choice of names. "I saw you staring."

Unable to argue with her logic and unwilling to encourage her, he returned to twisting his wedding ring around his finger, wondering how long it would be until he had the courage to remove it—if he ever removed it. The hollowness Miranda's death had created left him feeling as if he were half a man, held together only by a fragile thread that threatened to snap with every beat of his broken heart.

He heard the crinkle of paper next to him and, a second later, saw a pinch of dark crumbs fly through the air to land in front of a number of pigeons. Intrigued, he watched as they scrambled for the largest pieces, and he idly wondered what they ate when those who fed them died.

"Chocolate muffin," Tori said, not waiting for him to ask. "They love it. Usually people just feed them bread and seeds, you know, so I thought I'd change it up, give them some dessert."

"Aren't you afraid chocolate will harm the birds?" The question was out before he'd even realized he was asking it. She shrugged.

"They keep eating it, so it isn't killing them. If it is and they're stupid enough to eat it, then just call me Darwin."

Miranda would have never been so careless, he thought with surprising bitterness. She'd have done the research and consulted an avian expert to make sure she wasn't hurting them.

When he didn't respond, she gave him an odd look he could see in his peripheral, and she stared at his hands. "Recently married?"

He sighed inwardly. She wasn't going away, and the last thing he wanted right now was a conversation. Still, there was little choice in the matter; in order to escape her, he'd have to leave the bench, and there was no guarantee she wouldn't follow. The tightness in his chest showed no signs of disappearing either, so he resigned himself to both.

"Fifteen years ago," he said quietly, unable to look directly at her.

"Getting a divorce then?"

"No." Pursing his lips, he then took a deep breath and released it, trying to calm the tension that was rising within him again. He couldn't cry, not yet. "She died."

"Oh." Didn't she have any sort of propriety? Wasn't it obvious that he wanted to be alone? Instead of apologizing and moving away, she scooted closer. Daniel, already pressed up against the armrest, had nowhere else to go without leaving the bench. "That blows, I'm sorry."

"Yeah, me too," he all but whispered. What else was there to say but that? He certainly hadn't been able to think of anything in the days since Miranda had passed, when he'd been bombarded with condolences.

"When did she die?" Tori asked, her voice taking on a much more sympathetic tone.

"Three days ago," Daniel said, looking up from his hands to stare out across the pond. "Car accident."

"Were you driving?"

He shot her a stunned look. That was the first time anyone had asked. "No, I wasn't in the car," he finally said, having managed to gather his wits. "She was driving."

As if it'd been her fault. The moment the words left his lips, he instantly regretted them. "But it wasn't her fault," he added quickly. "There was a train and—and malfunctioning warning signals. Wasn't her fault at all."

"Never is, is it?"

Unsure of how to interpret her response, he opted to remain silent, having little desire to talk about that horrendous night. Opening the door to see two police officers standing in front of him, ready to tell him the bad news and offer their pity, was an image he'd never forget.

"Do you want to feed the pigeons?" Tori said after a few seconds had passed. She offered him the chocolate muffin, and he shook his head slightly, unable to bring himself to do it. That was something he'd only done with Miranda, something he thought he'd never bring himself to do again.

Not outwardly put off that he'd refused, Tori tore off another small piece of muffin and tossed the crumbs at the birds. "You should feed the pigeons," she said mildly. "They like it, you know, and it's good karma. Besides, it doesn't hurt anyone, does it? There's nothing wrong with spreading a little happiness every now and then."

Not quite willing to point out that birds, as far as he knew, didn't know what happiness was, Daniel shifted in his seat. He'd forgotten how uncomfortable the bench was.

"My boyfriend and I just broke up," Tori announced, as if he hadn't any clue about the ordeal she'd just experienced. He rather thought the whole park had heard the extensive fight between them, with the way he was yelling and she was screaming. "I've known him since we were tots—our mums are best friends, love the idea of their offspring having sprogs together."

As much as he hated receiving them, he could think of nothing else to say but to offer his condolences as well. "I'm sorry."

"Me too." She flashed him that catty grin again, and this time he didn't mind it so much. "He's quite a looker, you know. Got long blonde hair—I'm a sucker for long blonde hair, and he pulls it back into this tight little ponytail that drives me mad. Over a foot taller than me, too, did you see him?"

He shook his head, but he didn't think she noticed, as she continued to chat without tearing her eyes away from the pigeons.

"All the girls at university have been after him for years, but I sank my claws into him by the time we were twelve. Love of my life, he is."

"It's a shame, the way things turned out," Daniel said distractedly, his thoughts drifting back to Miranda. Two seconds one way or the other and she'd still be with him, still be breathing, and it would be another poor soul sitting next to Tori, who was undoubtedly only moments away from describing how her ex had been in bed.

"It is, isn't it?" she said thoughtfully, crumbling up another piece of muffin. He noticed she wasn't saving any for herself. "He's called Colin. I think you two would like each other. You look like a smart bloke, and he's top of our class at university."

Daniel made a small, noncommittal noise in the back of his throat as he once again stared out towards the pond. The blue-green waters were exactly the color of Miranda's eyes, and he'd told her so the first day they'd met.

"Want to know why I left him?"

He cocked his head slightly, knowing he was going to hear it either way.

"I left him because he looked at another girl the wrong way when we entered the park. Scanned her right in front of me and everything, the lousy git. It doesn't help that she was about a size negative ten and I'm—well, *not*. She was a bloody blonde, too, you know—well, of course you know, you're a bloke. Bet your wife was blonde, wasn't she?"

This time Daniel turned to scowl at her, hot anger rising inside of his already-tense body. It was the first strong emotion he'd felt other than grief in three days. Tori, however, didn't seem to notice, and was instead focused on the pigeons in front of them, not sparing Daniel a glance.

"But you know what?" she said, continuing on as if nothing were the matter. "It doesn't matter, because by the time he comes back round the park, I'm going to run up to him and hug him like I haven't seen him in years, and he's going to cover me in these wet, sloppy kisses he knows I love, and everything's going to be okay, because he's brilliant, you know, and I'd never leave him for anything."

Baffled, Daniel spoke without thinking, his voice tight and forced. "This—this is something you do then?"

"Nearly every weekend," she said with a firm little nod. "It gives us a little while to remember that we couldn't live without each other even if we tried. It'd be hell, you know, going on without him." This time she gave him her first sad look, and for a long moment their eyes locked. "I suppose you *would* know, wouldn't you?"

To that Daniel said nothing, too choked up to breathe, let alone speak. Her sad little smile continued even after she'd turned her attention back on the pigeons. He hadn't wanted to cry—couldn't cry, not yet, and here he was, on the brink of tears because of what a girl half his age was saying. It hit him that it was the truth, that he *did* know what it was like to lose the love of his life, and now he was going to have to face it every day. Miranda wouldn't be coming around the park for him like Colin would for Tori.

"She hasn't left you, you know," Tori said softly as she gathered the pieces of her half-gone muffin up and placed them back in the brown bag. "She's never going to leave you. It's up to you to never leave her."

As she stood, he noticed the man, Colin, coming back around the trail. When Daniel caught Tori's eye, he saw a beautiful, genuine grin, one that reminded him forcefully of Miranda. His own lips curled into a tiny smile, the best he could manage, and he gave her a nod, silently wishing her the best of luck. With a gleeful glint in her eyes, she skipped off, pouncing on Colin when she reached him some ten meters away. Daniel tried not to stare as the two embraced exactly as Tori said they would, and he wiped away a pair of tears that trickled down his cheek. He watched openly as they walked hand-in-hand out of the park, Tori leaning against Colin with a blissful expression on her pixie face.

It was then, once they were gone and Daniel was again alone, that he noticed she'd left the brown bag holding the muffin. He picked it up slowly, opening the bag with the sort of delicacy he used only with the most fragile of things. Pulling off a piece of the moist chocolate muffin, he gently rolled it between his fingers as it fell apart and onto the ground. The gray and pearl pigeons gathered around once more, cooing as they pecked at the crumbs nearest them. As another tear rolled down his cheek, a small, peaceful smile graced his lips and he decided Tori was right. Miranda hadn't left him, not when he could sit on the park bench, feeding the pigeons and still loving her. This was simply their walk around the park, and with each moment that passed, he would love her even more, eager for the day when she would be waiting for him on their bench.

They called her Colleen of Killarney,
The daughter of publican Barney.
Alas and alack!
Too much time on her back
Filled the girl up with far more than Blarney.

—Elizabeth George

The delights of Ireland, its generous and charming people, can be all summed up in a glass of their famous drink: a pint, or if you prefer, half a pint, of Guinness. It is presented carefully poured with a deep froth on top of a dark and mysterious liquid. The first taste leaves a comical ring of froth around the upper lip, an exterior sign of pleasures to come. Slowly as your thirst is quenched, some inexplicable desire compels you to turn to your drinking companions and tell them a story. Even when the glass is empty, there still remain signs of the telltale froth as a reminder of your Irish experience. If you look carefully into the bottom of the glass, maybe you will understand why Ireland has given the world so many great authors. Ah! If only writing a good story were as easy as enjoying a glass of Guinness!

COUNTERPOINT ON THE STREETS OF DUBLIN

by David Nutt

From across the street, the object in the store window looked huge and extremely ungainly. It took up the whole side of the shop's dirty front window, making it difficult to see what the item actually was. Before crossing the street, I noticed the shop's sign: *Antiques for all tastes!* It made me smile, as I could see the owner picking out the words from some modern marketing book, extolling the advantages of selling a broad range of merchandise.

I crossed the street and entered the store. In the corner by the window was a monstrous rococo object. It was a gigantic grandfather's clock, or maybe a more appropriate term would be a great-grandfather's clock, as it measured well over six feet. The clock was made from highly polished mahogany. Its face had an instant appeal with large Roman numerical numbering and a handsome pair of hands. On the lower half of the horologe's face was the word *London* written with such authority that nobody would forget that it came from that fair city. On the right side was a life size wooden carving of a young maiden clothed in flowing garments. The damsel was depicted looking wistfully out into the middle distance; she was leaning against the clock's base represented by a sculptured tree; at her feet were carved enchanting fairies dancing to the tunes of an elf musician. Above the horologe's face, a celestial gathering of angels looked down on this merry scene. Its baroque form engendered an extraordinarily magical and seductive ambiance. Any curious person would immediately wonder how it got there and who was the craftsman responsible for this preposterous piece.

I noticed a man, barely visible, at the back of the store listening to his portable phone. I moved toward him and signalled I would like to talk. He looked at me, threw up his hands and pointed to the speaking section of the phone. The person on the other end of the line was clearly enjoying the sound of his own voice. Patiently I waited. Minutes later, my patience was waning. The fellow stood just listening without saying a word. My next sign for attention was decidedly more aggressive. He looked at me again, threw up his hands but this time he placed the portable phone on a tabletop that was lying nearby and pushed on the speaker button. Instantly the back of the store was filled with the loud sound of a man's heavy Irish brogue talking about horse racing:

"Now we come to the 4.30 at Limerick this afternoon… Sean, my lad, it's a steal… Duke of Milan by miles… I sneaked into the horse's stable last night and saw him pissing, strong stuff… obviously very fit… he's got a pair of legs on him that a kangaroo would envy... What do you think…? Don't answer… I already agree with you… A steal… he will win by a mile…!"

The voice then moved on to the next race and started discussing the merits of two horses, systematically throwing out questions and supplying answers totally ignoring that somebody was on the other end. After a few minutes of entertaining stories about the health of certain horses, tidbits about trainers, jockeys and the flow of betting money, I interjected with a question about the clock.

At the other end of the line the voice boomed. "Did I hear you asking about the clock? Maggie's Farm was clocked running 8.4 seconds a furlong the last time she was out."

Turning to me, the storekeeper said, "You know it's solid mahogany and was made in England."

Before I could place another question, the voice interrupted, "Sean, my lad, you are wrong there, it is an Irish piebald horse."

Without a pause, the man on the other end of the phone started discussing racing at Downpatrick. This disturbing one-sided conversation continued at a lively pace. I thought I would try my luck just one more time so I asked the name of the clockmaker. The storekeeper never had a chance to reply. Loud and clear the question was answered. "The horse was sired out of Jazzy Dee and its mother was Miles go Metric, excellent pedigree, my lad."

As I left the store disgruntled, the older man called after me, "Come back in the afternoon. Mornings are impossible when there is racing."

I stopped in my tracks.

"Is there any day in Ireland when there is no racing?"

"You are right mate, very few."

Minutes later I was in a coffee shop; thoughts about the clock continued ticking in my brain. It was frustrating not being able to find out about its history. My time in Dublin was limited so I knew I could not return in the afternoon. *Tant pis!* as the French say.

Head bent and deep in concentration I continued my stroll through the small streets at the back of Trinity College when I heard the lyrical voice of a young Irish girl.

"Want to buy a heart?"

I looked up to be confronted with three charming young women dressed in a catchy clown's uniform enhanced with large white floppy collars. The whiteness of their ample collars had the delightful effect of highlighting their young fresh complexion. The sunlight's reflection on the white glittering cloth gave me the vivid impression that a spotlight had been turned on and a theatre's curtain had been raised.

"That's an interesting question." I laughingly replied. "Young maidens, what kinds of hearts have you for sale?"

The eldest, without doubt the prettiest, with a charming smile across her lips, was quick with her repartee: "Sir, we have a fine selection, what kind of heart would you be looking for?"

In replying, my voice portrayed a concerned tone. "Given my age, it would please me to have a young robust heart that will carry me the many miles I wish still to travel."

By this time I realized that these three young beauties had been contracted for the day to sell small red lapel badges for some Irish heart organization. But the initial exchange of words had placed us into the land of theatre, make believe, shamrocks and leprechauns. The young woman was obviously intent on keeping up this badinage.

"Ah! Sir, you are asking a lot, but let me take a look."

"While you are looking ask your young friends if they have a heart similar to Dorian Grey's for sale. This would indeed be a rare gift, wisdom from old age combined with the vigour of youth."

As they pretended to rummage in their baskets for my request, I had a disconcerting image of the many hearts that lay over the battlefields of Ireland. I saw hearts torn literally and metaphorically from Irish souls in the struggle and strife for human decency and the freedom of independence. I thought these three joyful young women, clearly at peace with the world, had a lot to thank their ancestors for.

I was taken out of my thoughts by the announcement that, after an exhaustive search, they believed they had come up with a heart that would satisfy the requirements of "sir's request".

The eldest member of the trio told me that their chosen heart belonged to a young man who recently had fatal car accident through no fault of his own. The tragedy was even more poignant as the accident had taken place two days before his marriage.

At this point I held up my hand.

"You want to sell me a heart surrounded by a disturbing history of this nature?"

"Sir, you don't understand. He went to his grave full of love, hope and ambition. What more could you ask for?"

Maybe it was their lyrical voices or the three attentive and engaging faces before me that, in an act of total surrender, I asked one of them to place the red button on my lapel while I searched my pockets for some money.

As I left, I doffed my imaginary cap to my fellow actors and the young ladies curtsied.

The way back to my hotel for lunch took me across Saint Stephen's Green. Spotting an empty seat on park bench I decided to take a rest. A man, holding a leash attached to a good-looking Irish setter, occupied the adjacent place. The dog was lying quietly, resting its head on its front paws, with the back end of its body extended under the bench. As the dog was positioned between his owner and the free space I asked,

"Mind if I sit here? Will it disturb your dog?" The tone of my voice was polite but firm.

The occupant of the seat was bent over reading a book that he held in his free hand so my question was directed to the top of a checked cloth cap. He looked up. I beheld the face of a man in his early thirties. His features were well formed and his cheeks and nose had just the right sprinkling of freckles as if some artist had carefully calculated the exact quantity needed for the finished portrait to be pleasing.

"Be my guest, but be careful not to touch the dog. He is disposed towards weird behavioural tendencies." The voice, as I had suspected, had the captivating sound of the Irish accent.

"Thank you, I will be careful. I know how dogs can be touchy if stepped on."

"Touchy if stepped on?" was the swift retort. "It is much worse than that. This animal is distinctly peculiar." He continued muttering, "Mind you it may be too early to judge, as I have only had *his lordship* a month."

I sat down, carefully avoiding any contact with the dog.

The dog was peacefully resting, gazing dreamily along the snout of its nose. The man continued to read his book. His remark about the animal being peculiar seemed strangely out of context with the present scene. I could not help requesting the owner to enlighten me on the dog's bizarre behaviour.

As he turned to face me, I noticed his visage had the luminous quality often seen on actors as they step into the spotlight.

"Oh! You want to hear my dog story?" His voice had acquired an enthusiastic tone and that appealing seductive sound, often belonging to a good storyteller.

"I would love to," I replied without hesitation. However over the years I have heard a few shaggy-dog stories, and I have never found them very appealing.

He closed his book, made a swivelling movement with his lower body so that he was facing me, adjusted his cap, and began:

"I knew it the moment I walked in the front door late one night. The fierce aggressive shine in the dog's eyes said it all. 'How could you, how could you not take me out today?' I took one more look to make sure I was reading the message correctly. There was no mistake. Ears at half- mast, head slightly cocked to one side as if the silly dog knew what a question mark was.

"All right, it can happen once in a while," I said addressing the dog in a soothing tone.

The dog's head moved to the other side, the question mark position still in place.

"I forgot. You are right, I didn't take you out the day before yesterday. I am sorry but I have been busy. Tonight, for instance, I had a date with my girl friend." In a lower register, almost a whisper, I continued, "actually she does not like dogs."

The reaction was immediate; the dog backed off three paces, muscles tensed as he eased himself on his haunches in a pouncing position. From there he just stared at me. I had the horrible feeling he was meditating on his next move. His gaze intensified.

"Look," I said addressing the dog. "Surely between good friends I can be forgiven. Let me make you your favourite dinner dish."

This carefully placed attempt of extending an olive branch had no effect; he just continued to fix a piercing stare in my direction.

Gosh, I thought to myself, this dog is having a weird behavioural attack. I had vaguely heard that certain dogs subjected to emotional stress could do strange things. I also seemed to remember that under these circumstances, you should immediately pet the animal and make sweet noises. I moved forward, the dog growled, and gave me a final penetrating stare before leaving the room.

"Well, my lad, with that attitude you aren't going to get your special dinner," I hurled after him.

I never saw the dog again that night, but as a small gesture of reconciliation I left him some stale biscuits in his bowl. That will teach him.

The next morning, I awoke to the aroma of coffee, eggs and bacon. Funny... I didn't remember leaving a set of front door keys with my girlfriend. I was even more surprised to find that my clothes were not on my night chair.

Oh! I must have left her a set of keys. Ha! Ha! Breakfast in the nude, the little lassie is more adventurous that I thought.

Naked, I tiptoed into the kitchen for the big surprise. I was horrified to see the dog, in an upright position, hind legs extended, crouched over the stove with my treasured omelette pan in his right paw. On hearing me, the dog moved his paw and flipped over the eggs, turned and barred his teeth at the same time, sending vicious growls in my direction.

Instinctively, I am embarrassed to say, I fell on my hands and knees. How I regretted those stale biscuits! Every time I moved, his growl intensified. I was obliged to stay in this ridiculous posture until the dog had finished breakfast. Finished breakfast is not quite correctly stated: the scraps from his plate were thrown on the floor for me.

Then the dog left the kitchen.

He was back a few minutes later dragging a basket of clothes with his leash carefully laid on top. There was no argument.

"What did people say about dogs being weird?"

"I remember cringing as I heard my neighbour call out. "Pleasant day for walking the dog!" *His lordship* was in front of me, ears at full mast, tail at attention, stepping forward as if nothing had happened.

At this point the narrator took off his cap revealing a healthy head of red hair through which he swiftly ran his right hand. "It's a rum situation. What do you think?"

As I didn't believe his story, I could not resist the following observation. "I am surprised your dog knew which one was your favourite omelette pan."

As my words sank in, I detected a slightly pained expression on his face.

"Be serious, this is no laughing matter. Since that time my girlfriend has given me up, and I have sleeping difficulties."

I sat there perplexed: Was this one of those Irish stories that leaps from reality to fiction as quickly as elves jump over toadstools or, in this enchanting land of leprechauns, could it be truth? It is said that behind every closed door and window in Ireland there is a story to be told. The dog's owner looked genuinely concerned, but did I detect a great actor's performance? I still found it hard to believe. Try and imagine a dog cooking breakfast!

Carefully measuring my words and playing along with a sympathetic approach to his dilemma, I said. "You know, maybe an admirable idea is that you don't take your dog out for a couple of days and see if he reacts in the same way. It might be just one of those odd moments in life when there is no sane explanation."

"My friend, that is exactly what I intend on doing."

At this moment the dog raised its head and focused its eyes on my face.

I could have sworn it winked at me!

∾

While walking the streets of Dublin, I ran into a woman begging, holding her nine-year-old son. I asked if I could pay her for an interview. She was agreeable, so I asked her about her situation and her life. The story "Lost and Found" comes from information she provided that I further developed.

LOST AND FOUND
by Dani Brown

The boy's stomach churned as he heard sirens race up behind him and his friend, Anya Koslov, as they walked along College Street in front of Trinity College in Dublin.

They blended in with the throng of students headed to the first classes of the day. Anya's tall slim build, long black hair and haunted dark eyes made her appear older than her thirteen years. Laurence, at ten, was slightly shorter than Anya and had shaggy blonde hair. He wore torn jeans, an old coat and carried a tattered backpack. Neither went to school, they were both students of the street. Gardá cars, blue lights flashing, flew past them and whipped into the entrance of Trinity College.

Laurence pushed through the crowds that milled around them to be further from the street and closer to the ancient stone wall that surrounded the school. He worried that if the Gardá saw his face, they would know of the crime that had forced him and his mother to flee London. Since they had moved to Dublin, life had improved in some ways but the fear remained. Fear of the London police was now replaced by fear of the Irish Gardá.

Anya joined Laurence by the wall and grabbed him by the shoulder. "Are you okay? You're shaking."

Anxiously, he glanced back at the college. He saw two Gardá officers come out of a building and look down the crowded sidewalk at him. "They found me." Laurence's heart raced, sweat formed on his forehead, as he pulled away from Anya.

"Are you sick?" Anya called.

Laurence darted away through the crowd, toward Grafton Street where cars couldn't follow.

Anya followed him as he zig-zagged around the tourists encumbered with bags. She grabbed at the back of Laurence's heavy coat, forcing him to stop. "Who found you?" she asked panting.

"The Gardá. I have to find a place to hide. " Laurence shook off his friend and raced forward, glancing to the left and right for a hiding place. There was no relief in sight.

Only people, cars, and an endless array of storefronts bordering the street. *Too bad there were so many cars,* he thought, eyeing a manhole cover in the middle of the road. The tunnels below Dublin had given him refuge from the Gardá before.

"Let's go back to your apartment," Anya said.

Laurence stopped and shook his head as Anya reached his side. "They'll find Mum, it's my fault."

"Your fault?"

"Tell Mum what happened."

"I don't know what happened." Anya said plaintively

"Tell her the Gardá saw me... I'm okay...Please." He looked behind him. He didn't see the police anymore but knew he needed to hide. He needed to protect his mother from his mistake. He would be a better man than his da had been.

Laurence sprinted down the street into St. Stephen's Green. As he rounded the corner, he saw Anya had stopped and sat on a bench. He raced around clumps of people picnicking on the grass and threaded his way through park benches where others were eating lunch. Finally he reached the back of the park. Sirens wailed from the road. Laurence ducked under some bright green bushes. Rain, captured in the leaves, fell on his face as he stood and ran down the trail between the stone wall and the tall hedges. His ankles became damp where there were no socks.

When he reached the corner, he dropped to the cool damp ground and pressed his back against a tall stone wall. As he tucked his knees up to his chest he said a prayer that God's will would be done. Maybe it was time that he paid for the crime he had committed. Tears began to fall as he thought of his mother; he brushed them away. If he turned himself in, then his mother would be safe. He wouldn't tell them where she was. Still, he should tell her goodbye and try to explain.

His decision made, he looked at his surroundings.

The wall behind him was covered with moss. As he moved, the dense foliage above him baptized him with more drops of water. He noticed a large log lying on its side covered with rotting leaves. Except for wild daisies, the rest of the Green was manicured. Maybe the groundskeepers didn't care about what they couldn't see. Curious, Laurence leaned forward and easily brushed the leaves off the log.

Laurence ran his fingers over the surface of the back of the log and was surprised to find a hole that had something sticking out of it. He pressed his back against the wall, bent up his knees, took a deep breath and pushed as hard as he could. One end of the log shifted far enough out from the wall that he could reach behind it. His fingers felt something smooth and hard. He pulled the heavy object out. It was a leather bag with buckles.

The last time he had given his mother a bag like this one, she had sold it to buy him a used coat for his tenth birthday. He hoped whatever was in it wouldn't be something she would sell. Clutching the bag, he closed his eyes and drifted into a fitful sleep. When he awoke he peeked out through the hedge and saw that it was getting darker. Only a few people remained in the park. Laurence hadn't heard any sirens in a while and didn't see any Gardá. He stood, and hefted the leather bag to his shoulder.

He exited the Green, on York Street where he and his mother lived with his aunt in her apartment. He hoped he would find Anya in the basement where he had first met her, six months before.

The brick apartment building was deserted outside. Most of the elderly residents didn't want to be out after dark. He ran down chipped concrete steps to the basement and through the damp, dimly lit rooms. As the dank air enveloped him, he zipped his coat. Rounding a corner, he ducked under some pipes, brushed cob webs out of his way, and tapped softly on the door to the tunnels.

"Anya," he whispered.

The door opened a crack.

"It's me," he murmured urgently.

Anya stepped though the door and into the shadows that played on the wall from the light bulb in the staircase.

She hugged Laurence. "I'm glad you're safe. I told your mum what you asked me to."

"Is she okay?"

"She's worried, but said you were a smart boy."

"Look what I found!"

"What is it? Perhaps you could give it to your mum for Mother's Day."

"I thought so too," Laurence dropped to the ground and invited Anya to join him. He cradled the bag in his lap as he began to unbuckle the straps. Reaching inside he pulled out something that was large and rectangular wrapped in a dirty rag. Under that was a heavy plastic, and beyond that was a paper wrap.

Inside was an old book. It was pretty, but the colors were faded. The cover had a picture of a person holding a child and there were two people in the corners above him that had halos and wings. He began to look through the thick yellow pages of the book. A corner crumbled off in his hand.

"Be careful…it looks old."

Laurence pointed at one of the pages "A cross!"

"Maybe a book of faith from some priest. Where did you find it?"

"In the bushes at the Green."

Anya knelt down beside him. "Let me have a look, will ya?"

"Here," Laurence turned the book toward her as she sat down next to him.

"I've not seen a book so big before."

Anya leaned closer to the book as it sat on Laurence's

lap. "I don't understand the words…must be from far away or a time long past."

"The pictures are pretty."

"Yes… but it's getting late, your mum will worry. Be off now. I hope she likes her Mum's Day gift."

Laurence ran up the dark staircase surrounded by the odor of urine. He stepped on a hypodermic syringe and stumbled, but caught himself and continued down the shadowy hallway toward the apartment where he and his mother lived. He was proud he could be a better man than his father and give his mother a beautiful gift. Father hadn't even given them food. He had wasted all his money on the ponies. Still, his mother had always found him enough to eat. She had also used her body to shield him from his father's wrath. Today it was Mum's Day and he hadn't had a bloody thing to give her…until now.

He pushed open the door to the tiny flat. A bare light bulb hanging from the ceiling was the only bright spot in the room. He dropped the bag containing the book just inside the door as he closed and locked it behind him.

Panting, he glanced around the room for his mother. She sat bundled in an old grey wool blanket by the window, looking down at the street. Her feet were tucked under the blanket; a knit cap kept her head warm.

"I was worried about ya, luv. Come here," she said.

"I found something for ya."

Laurence crossed the room to his mother and knelt at her feet, placing the damp leather bag in her lap. "It's about God. There's angels."

She stroked his face. "You are such a love. I'd not be wanting to live without ya."

Tears filled her eyes.

"We're safe Mum. Da can't hurt us anymore."

His mother opened the bag and looked at the beautiful book it contained. Horns honked on York street below the apartment. The streetlights outside the window cast eerie shadows on the wall.

"My, what a pretty thing. Thank ya, love. You've not been

where you shouldn't have been have you? Not taken what wasn't yours, have ya?"

"I found it in the bushes, Mum."

She hugged him gently, "It is just lovely, but I worry what you done in London will catch you one day. You need to stay clear of the Gardá here.

"I couldn't bear to see him hit ya again. When he came after ya with the board I had to stop him, I did." Laurence's voice began to quaver.

His mother hugged him tightly. "Shush. It's done. It was by accident."

"What if he comes back from hell?"

"That he shan't do my luv. Have I not told ya that God will protect us?"

"Why didn't God protect us before?"

"It's not right for the likes of us to question our Lord."

"I have scary dreams, Mum…"

"I know, luv, I hear you cry out and I pray for you to find peace. But you must find your own way."

"The Ten Commandments say thou shalt not kill," Laurence said as he moved to his pallet by the wall and settled under the blankets.

"The Bible says one can when it is necessary to protect those who believe in Jesus."

Laurence fell silent but found new strength in his mother's words. He was glad they were alone, grateful that his aunt had gone to visit someone in Kilkenny.

He had not spoken with his mother about his father since they had left London. Maybe God would forgive him. Maybe the book was a sign of God's forgiveness. He watched his mother as she turned the pages of the book and smiled. A few minutes later, she set the book on the table, and pulled the chain below the bulb, leaving only shadows from the street lights to dance on the walls. Laurence heard her move across the room and settle onto the old couch with the spring poking out, the fabric worn away in spots. He knew she deserved better.

"Try not to worry too much, my luv."

Laurence knew he needed to talk to his mother about going to the Gardá and turning himself in. But, right now he enjoyed seeing his mother happy.

As he drifted off to sleep he saw his mother smiling as she danced among the pretty pictures in the book he had given her.

The next morning, Laurence checked the basement for Anya. He didn't find her there so he headed to the open air market. Streetlights automatically dimmed as the sun rose. It was cool but dry, the air fresh from the previous night's rain. Laurence whistled as he glanced around at the stores not yet open. Everything seemed brighter today. His mother had looked so peaceful on the couch this morning that he hadn't had the heart to wake her and tell her that he was turning himself in to the Gardá. Maybe he wouldn't after all. As he passed the flower stalls, he smiled at the gray-headed proprietor. She smiled back and handed him a wilted flower.

"Thank ya. Have ya seen Anya?"

"Back a the alley," the old woman said, as she pointed down the street and to the right.

Laurence trotted past the vegetable and fruit stands being filled by the old grocer that still used a horse and cart to carry his wares. Turning into the alley, Laurence spotted Anya sitting on an old crate. She was munching on a muffin. "Hello."

Laurence's stomach growled as he watched her eat.

"Hungry? Have half mine." Anya broke the muffin in half, crumbs fell to the ground as she handed his half to him.

Laurence grabbed the muffin and chewed.

"Men, they are all so greedy." Anya said laughing.

Laurence smiled down at Anya on the old plastic crate. "What do you know of men?"

"More than I can tell. Things boys do not need to know."

"Secrets. I have secrets, too."

"Tell me." Anya stood. "Don't ya trust me? My brother Ivan told me all his secrets."

Laurence looked away and shuffled his feet. Anya began to walk out of the alley to the street. When Laurence caught up with her, he saw tears in her eyes.

"Don't cry," he pleaded.

"You remind me so much of my brother Ivan...such a handsome boy...and so smart."

"What happened to your family?"

"I do not know. The men from the agency told my family that I was being taken to America and that when I had made enough money that I could send for them. Before Perestroika, my family did well. Afterward, not so. "

"Why are you here?"

"The men lied to me and my family. I was not allowed to keep any of the money I had earned, or allowed to go home"

"Who are you hiding from?"

"That I cannot tell you. They would kill you just for being my friend."

"Why?"

Anya sighed heavily and wiped away her tears. "They say that the money they gave my family means they own me. The time I spent with those men and their friends was not good. I was made to do things their wives would not do. So I ran away. That's all I will say."

Anya looked down the street at a full trash can. "The trash collectors haven't been round yet. Maybe there is a newspaper. Would you like me to read to you?"

Laurence ran to the metal trash container and began to dig for breakfast. "Look," he crowed triumphantly, "Someone left most of a croissant with cheese and egg, there's a bottled soda too."

"What about something to read?" Anya asked joining him.

Laurence handed her a wet newspaper from under the bottom of a dribbling cola bottle.

"Here."

"Breakfast, and something to read. We are lucky." Anya looped her arm with Laurence's as they walked down another alley that the pair often frequented. The ground outside the door to the tunnels was still damp from the previous day's rain.

Anya began to sit but Laurence grabbed her arm.

"Sit on my coat," Laurence said as he removed his coat and placed it on the ground at Anya's feet.

She looked down at Laurence and smiled. "Thank you. That's sweet. Most of the men I have known were not *gentle* men."

"Da wasn't a gentleman," Laurence took a deep breath. "He didn't treat my Mum like a lady."

"What happened to your da?"

Laurence bit his lip and balled his fists. "I...killed him... He was beating Mum with a board. He threw it down and then tried to choke her. I picked up the board and hit him. I didn't mean to kill him but he was choking Mum."

Anya patted the cracked concrete next to her and looked up at him. "It was an accident; you were protecting your Mum. You should be honored for it."

Laurence brushed away tears that had sprung to his eyes, and sat next to her.

She turned to the comics and began to read. After a few minutes, Anya handed the paper to Laurence.

"Now it's your turn." Anya placed her arm around his shoulders and smiled.

"I like it when you read."

"And I love to read to ya. But I'm about you learning to read. The teacher at my school in Russia taught me to read English. She said I could get a job as a tour guide if I could read English . I would make more money than if I went to University. What does your Mum say about you learning to read?"

"She's says I am going to be a better man than my da if I learn to read."

"All the more reason you'll not be getting out of reading that easy. The government will pay for you to go to college if you can read."

"How do you know?"

"I heard people talk. They also say that you can earn a good wage if you have been to University. Not like Russia. In Russia they value intellect but do not want to pay you for it. Better to guide tourists. One day I will go home and help my family by showing people St. Petersberg." She paused.

"Now read that one," Anya pointed to a comic strip with only five pictures and one or two words in each bubble. As the boy struggled with each word, Anya murmured words of encouragement.

"Now, let's have a go at something a little harder." Anya flipped the pages until she reached the front page.

Laurence carefully read the headline, not wanting his teacher and friend to think he hadn't been paying attention to the lessons she had been giving him. "Book."

"Good," Anya said, nodding her head encouragingly as she looked down the alley, always watchful for those who believed they owned her.

"of ...Kells...Stolen" Laurence sounded out while Anya nodded absentmindedly as she watched the people that walked by.

Laurence looked at Anya. "What is a book of Kells?"

"I don't know. Have they a picture at the bottom of the page?" Anya asked as she flipped the page up to see the lower half.

They gasped at the same time. Anya snatched the paper and began to read the article out loud.

BOOK OF KELLS STOLEN

Last night while Dublin slept, one of their priceless antiquities was removed from its case at Trinity college. The Book of Kells, written by monks in the eighth century, contains the best example of illuminations or drawings of that period. It is the four gospels beginning with Matthew, written in Latin script in the Gaelic language. The Gardá believe that the thieves had help from someone who knew the alarm code as the alarm had been turned off. Cameras show the back of one of the thieves before he fled the scene. He is described as approximately 6'2" with a heavy build. In the photo he is seen handing the Book of Kells to someone out of the view of the camera. A ransom note has been received. The police report that the thieves claim to have hidden the book close to Trinity College. They also believe that the theft was due in part to a desire to humiliate the Gardá. A reward of 10,000 euro is being offered to any one with information leading to the arrest of the thieves or the recovery of the Book of Kells.

"You have to take the book back," Anya said.

"You do it."

"I can't, the Gardá know the men who took me from my family. They would give me back to them."

"Mum won't let me go to the Gardá."

"Killing your da was an accident and you're just a boy. The reward could help you and your Mum."

"Yes, and you too. You could go home to your family." Laurence jumped to his feet, snatched the paper from Anya's hands and ran down the street. But at home, his mother didn't want him to go to the Gardá. She worried for his safety, and said that no amount of money was worth losing her son.

Laurence argued that she had always told him to do what was right, even if it wasn't easy. They didn't even know if his father had been found. Dead bodies in their old London apartment building weren't really that unusual.

They finally decided to go to the Gardá station together and that Mother would do the talking. They wrapped the book in the old rag Laurence had found it in and placed the book in a paper bag.

Upon their arrival at the Gardá station, they were met by a burly man dressed in a dark uniform and a bright yellow vest.

"What are the likes of you doing here?" he asked.

Mother took a deep breath before she spoke. "Sir, we need to see someone bout something we found."

The officer glared at Laurence's mother. Laurence balled his fists in this pocket. He wanted to hit the officer but had promised his mother that he would be quiet.

"Madam, there is nothing any one here would be interested in from the likes of you and that boy." He glanced down at Laurence and sneered.

"Sir, please if you will—" Laurence's mother held out the bag to the officer

"We deal with things of importance here. The Book of Kells has been stolen. But what would you know of that? Probably can't even read, and have no idea what the Book of Kells is."

"Sir?"

"Off with ya now, we haven't the time."

As Mother pulled on Laurence's arm, the bag broke and the rag-covered book tumbled to the ground. They looked at each other and began to quickly walk away.

They heard the officer shout at them. Laurence looked at his mother.

"You decide," she said.

Laurence stopped. He turned. Standing tall, he walked toward the Gardá officer. His mother did not move.

Reaching the officer, Laurence looked up at the flat brown eyes and the lips that were drawn into a tight line.

"Here boy. Don't leave your dirty laundry with us, we'll burn it with the other trash." The policeman thrust the book wrapped in rags back into Laurence's hands. Laurence took a deep breath, looked up at the officer, then down at the package that he held.

Gulping, he spoke, "Sir, I think this is the book you're looking for."

The next morning, the Dublin paper carried the following front page article:

MODERN DAY RAGS TO RICHES STORY

Yesterday, Laurence Stocking, age 10, turned The Book of Kells in to the Gardá. As luck would have it , the reward for the Book of Kells' safe return was raised to 25,000 euro just hours before he presented it. When asked what he would do with the reward, the boy said that he would use the money to rent a better apartment for himself and his mother and to help a friend return to her family in Russia. He also dreams of one day attending University. During the Gardá interview, Laurence was absolved of the theft but informed the Gardá that he had killed his father in their London flat while defending his mother and wanted to pay his due for that mistake. The Gardá report that after talking to the police in London, no charges will be filed, as the death of the boy's father had been ruled accidental. They do, however, plan to continue the investigation into the theft of the book.

Sometimes it does pay to do the right thing.

Studying the history of Norway and Ireland resulted from my recent interest in genealogy. Other than where I live in Canada, my favourite place in all the world is Maui, Hawaii. We visit annually. At the Maui Writers Retreat and Conference in 2001 I experienced a "What If" seminar. Expecting this same format to be part of the Ireland Retreat experience, I thought, What if Norwegian trolls accompanied the early explorers up the River Liffy when Dublin was established, and another Norwegian troll settled on Maui with the immigrant workers? What if immigrant little people pairing with local little people contribute to a multiethnic population of little ones?

LITTLE FRIENDS IN IRELAND
by Myrtle Forberg Siebert

With palpable fear of discovery, I waited impatiently for an oportunity to zip open Shannon's travel bag a crack and squeeze out. All of the Tullius's travel bags were lined up on the sidewalk and the cab driver was busy unloading the larger suitcases when I made my escape. It had been a long journey from Hawaii in a very cramped space. Shannon and John Tullius had gone into the Westbury Hotel lobby to check in. Without much difficulty, I found the dark tunnels under the city of Dublin that I had read about. So that is how a menehune from Maui, Hawaii, came to be in Dublin, Ireland.

It didn't take long to find the below-ground hangouts of the Dublin 'little people' and within an hour I met a delightful female troll who says she is descended from traveling companions of early Viking explorers. We shared a table in a 'little people' pub beneath the city. I introduced myself as Koko, from Hawaii, and she told me her name was Nell. Over several pints of Guinness she told me her story, not unlike my own. Wouldn't you know, while the Maui writers were out scouring the city of Dublin for stories to write about, I have already discovered a real story on my very first evening in Ireland.

I began by telling Nell my own story. "My grandfather was a troll born in Norway. He came along with Halvor Johansen aboard the ship *Musca,* much like your ancestor arrived in Ireland many years earlier. Soon after the ship landed, my troll grandfather found the place where the menehune—as the 'little people' of Hawaii are called—played when their work was done. Approaching them, he introduced himself as Hans and they welcomed him into their circle.

"You see, a menehune is not much different from a troll, and is in fact, a lot like all other 'little people' around the world. Some are grumpy, some light-fingered, and most have a mischievous streak, but they all love to have a good time when they get together. Well, just look at me," I told her. "Then, of course, all little people share the same affection for human children." Although people can't see us, we are a visible reality to a child.

"Well, you see, Maui needed workers for the fields in 1881. Times were very bad in all the Scandinavian countries, so six hundred workers from Norway, Sweden, and Denmark signed up to come. Two ships landed at MacGregor Point, near the lighthouse just off Maalaea Bay on Maui, and my grandfather, Hans, went ashore.

"Many of the Norwegian immigrants to Maui weren't prepared for the kind of rough, hard work they were called upon to do in Hawaii, because most of them were artisans or had some manner of skills. They simply rebelled. The Norwegians—stubborn people they tend to be—and I can say that because I know them well, quickly gained a reputation for being troublemakers. Later in 1881, one of them even led the first worker's strike on the island. But I'm getting ahead of myself.

"Grandpa Hans had arrived with Halvor Johansen, one of those contract workers who came to Maui. Within a year, all but a hundred of the original Scandinavian group had left in disappointment. They had found conditions of working and living there impossible, but Halvor Johannsen had found a job in a market that made better use of his merchant experience. It wasn't long before he met a Hawaiian girl and settled down in a home on the side of the mountain, an extinct volcano known as Haleakala.

"Believing there could be a good future on Maui for him, too, my Grandpa Hans discovered a vacant home in the lava block fence that marked Halvor's property. Grandpa had already met a pretty menehune maid that he really liked. Named Lea, she had thick long dark hair and a winning smile as sweet as her personality. Once Grandpa Hans made the decision to stay, Lea and Hans were married.

"When I was still very young, Grandpa Hans told me about his first year on Maui. He said he had been determined to learn more of the menehune legends, especially since he was marrying a menehune girl. Grandpa paid attention whenever the term menehune was mentioned. One day a tour bus passed by and he could hear the tour leader explain, 'You see those high lava fences dividing the fields and keeping the cattle in place? That's an example of menehune workmanship,' he explained. 'You'll see their fences and watering places for the cattle built all over this side of the island. Menehune always work after dark so that's why you don't see them, but we who live on Maui couldn't manage without their help.'

"Scrounging through the books in Halvor's home one night after everyone had gone to bed, Grandpa Hans found an encyclopedia. This is what the book said:

> Menehune are craftsman, predominately stonemasons, each specializing in a distinct handicraft. The legends claim that the Menehune built temples, fishponds, and even highways. They make canoes, build houses, and do many of the pleasant things fairies are always doing. It is also told that when the ancestors of today's native Hawai'ians arrived on the islands, they found dams, temples and other structures built by the Menehune, who lived in caves.

"One day the merchant that Halvor Johansen worked for decided to sell the business and retire, so Halvor would be out of a job. Halvor's offer to buy was accepted and that was how he came to own the market where he had been working. Like any good Norwegian entrepreneur, Halvor and his wife set about increasing its size and modernity.

"Working after dark and, of course, unobserved, Grandpa Hans assisted them by moving lumber and other building supplies to locations that would make the job easier the next day. After the reconstruction was finished, Hans and Lea started their family.

"As more children were born to the Johansens, my grandparents found themselves increasingly busy. Hans helped restock shelves after the staff had gone home, and then he and Lea soothed the children when they awoke in the night. Everyone was kept busy. During occasional free time, Hans and Lea did volunteer work credited to menehunes all over the Hawaiian Islands.

"Grandpa Hans wanted to have a family of his own and in the fullness of time, Lea bore a tiny girl. That child was my mother." This was the first time I had admitted to Nell that I am of mixed ethnicity and Nell had a lot of questions about what that meant. "I am really more like a menehune, but I cherish my troll origin because without my grandpa's courage to travel, I would not be of Maui."

Nell's questions answered, I continued. "My father was part of a ring of menehunes who lived near Paia, that little village on the windward side, known for giant surfing waves. Paia is where windsurfers and boardsailers hang out. Since the sixties, the place has had a reputation for drug users, hippies and hangers on, but during the last fifteen years it has been cleaned up a lot. Redevelopment of some of the original buildings and addition of a variety of businesses have helped make it an attractive tourist destination.

"Both my menehune parents loved to party more than a little, and they eventually found themselves caught up in the relaxed attitudes of Paia. I don't know for certain, but I've assumed it was some negative influence they found there, and maybe the drugs that were part of the lifestyle contributed to their premature death.

"So here I was, an orphan at ten, and I needed to find a new place to be. I returned to the hillside where my elderly grandparents still lived. The Johansens had moved their business to Lahaina and bought a new home near the town. Only a year later, after my grandparents died within six months of each other, I discovered the Tullius family. Their home was in the same neighbourhood and I decided to make myself useful to them.

"I have really enjoyed living with them and making sure their daughter, Somer, was safe and happy. Somer is gone away to school now but she and I are still close in our hearts, as any child is when they have been raised among 'little people.'" Nell and all other 'little people' I've met in Dublin recognize the special connection they have with children, so I didn't have to elaborate on that part.

"I help the other menehunes at night when there is a large project to complete but really worthwhile jobs are few and far between these days. One good opportunity presented itself last January when our menehune gang heard about the rediscovery of the site where the original Scandinavian immigrant workers had landed. Some of their human descendents and supporters decided to move the monument—which in Norwegian is called *bautastein*—to a place that is more accessible for viewers.

"Since my troll ancestor was aboard one of those ships, it seemed right that I should help with the restoration. For the next month we dedicated spare time on the dark nights to our effort. When it was all finished, the Maui News ran an interesting story about the 125th anniversary celebration of those immigrants. I read that paper and finally understood the greater significance of our renewal project. The inscription on the monument told the story.

"But you must still be wondering what gave me the idea of coming to Ireland," I said to Nell. "Well, early in 2006 John and Shannon Tullius began talking about taking a Maui Writers group to Ireland. John is the recognized leader of the Maui

Writer's Conference held on Maui every year during the Labor Day weekend.

"I heard John say he would land in Dublin. It's a place I knew had originally been settled by Norsemen because that was one of Grandpa Hans's many stories about where some of his troll ancestors had gone to live. It occurred to me this might be a convenient travel opportunity, particularly when I had no living relatives and I'm still single.

"If trolls had come to Ireland with those first Norwegians, maybe their Norsk descendents still lived in Dublin. And here you are, just as I suspected. Besides, it seemed likely that other little people lived in Ireland. I had heard about one group called leprechauns. Then too, if my Norwegian troll grandfather had the courage to leave his home and travel for weeks across the seas, I should be able to endure a plane ride that would take less than a day. So when the Maui Writer's Conference people made plans to take a group of writers and wannabe writers to Ireland, I decided this was my chance to at least get closer to my ancestral home."

I had even wondered if I could find my way to Norway from Ireland, it being so much closer to Norway than Maui. Nell and I have had a wonderful time together, and she introduced me to all the little people she knew. I've met fairies, leprechauns, brownies, a few *nissen* and of course other trolls beside Nell. We talked and sang together with them and occasionally got up to some mischief. None of it hurt any of the human population but certainly established the fact that we were about.

One quiet night after the Maui Writers group had moved on to a new location for their second writing assignment and most of us had decided to take a break from the partying and nonsense, Nell and I observed a sad-looking older brownie come into the pub where we were having our dinner. He appeared to need some cheering so we invited him to sit with us.

I introduced Nell and provided a shortened version of my own story, and Nell explained that her ancestors had lived in Ireland for many years. We asked him how he came to be in Dublin that evening and he said his name was Ross, and he had come south in search of a wife. As the night progressed and other little people gathered around, part of his story came out. It was a very long story and we interrupted to ask questions or compare his experiences to our own.

Ross is descended from the good-natured, but often mischievous, little people of Scotland called brownies. Ross's great-grandparents came to Ireland from Scotland about 1825 with Sam and Anna Lundy. He had heard many stories about the 'old country,' but we were all interested in Ross's more recent history before he came to Dublin. Ross intimated that he had found the 'troubles' in Northern Ireland very tiresome and, although not dangerous for him personally, his family had lived with humans of the Protestant faith and that it had caused constant friction for them.

He told us that his great-grandparents had settled with the Lundys on a small farm in County Armagh and helped the family as good and loyal brownies for all the time the Lundys lived there. Through the births of the Lundy's children they continued serving the Scottish family. Nights became increasingly busy and it seemed there was no end to the workload.

Conditions became increasingly difficult in Northern Ireland of 1840 and Sam and Anna prepared to move once more. Stories of a better life in Canada had reached them. Sam's cousin had already made the move to Ontario and so they began to pack again. This time his great- grandparents dug in their heels and absolutely refused to set sail again.

Nell chimed in with something her grandparents had told her. The 'little people' of Nordic origin from whom she was descended had made the same decision centuries earlier not to return across the sea. Ireland was now their home.

"Sam and Anna Lundy and their children were eventually safely on board a ship in Belfast departing for Canada," Ross continued. The story of their leaving had been retold and passed down through the generations. "You know the Lundy children, ages 15, 11, 9 and 7 they were, had always been surrounded by brownies and other 'little people' so while the idea of getting on board a ship was frightening enough, having to do so without the comfort of their little brownie friends made it all much worse. They had no expectation of finding 'little friends' in the new world.

"We may be entirely invisible to unbelieving adults but we are certainly a reality to children. Setting the best example for the younger ones he knew how, John Lundy followed his father forward and poor James, biting his lower lip trying so hard to be brave, held Hugh's hand, but the youngest little Anne Jane pulled at her mother's skirts as Anna strode purposefully up the ramp and on to the deck. As the huge ship pulled away from the Belfast dock, crying and mournful wailing came from the children waving frantically through spaces at the rails."

After their people departed, Ross's great-grandparents needed to find a new family to live with. The wife pointed out a young couple with an oversized trunk being met by an agent at the dock. Perhaps a good home could be found with these people. And so it was that a new family home was established on the outskirts of Belfast and a brownie couple moved in, too. Ross went on to describe an age-old brownie test that's been used for centuries to determine a worthy family, saying it always feels good to demonstrate brownie mischief.

"We are a 'little people' who like to live in very tidy spaces. When human people arrive at their new home they are usually just too tired to unpack much. They may place the parcels and boxes in the correct rooms but it is generally very late and most often they simply make a bed and go to sleep. This is when we set to work.

"Even if the place is disorganized, we can make a better mess, is our attitude. So when a new family is asleep, we move their things around to the wrong rooms and mix up the packages so everything is really muddled when they awake in the morning. Having no appreciation of what the brownie has done, worthy humans simply began again the next morning to organize their things.

"It may take them some time to settle in to a new home

and make all their belongings tidy and orderly, just the way a brownie would want his adopted home to be. Then late at night, after the household is quiet again, a room check is completed in the best brownie tradition. If we approve and their work is meticulous, we will become an unseen loyal resident helper. If not, we move on, looking for a different set of humans who can pass our test."

On his way from Belfast to Dublin, Ross took his time, stopping in different homes along the way to see if they had a resident brownie or fairy suitable to be his wife. Along the way he had encountered many leprechauns, but always the story was the same, they were all male.

"Why is that?" he asked the assembled 'little people,' and there appeared to be no answer from any of us. Only a few days after arriving, I had met several leprechauns. "They seem to be fun-loving, good-natured little men," Ross continued. "After asking around, I learned they usually live in farmhouses and wine cellars. Although they drink a lot, they sometimes do special chores for humans. It is widely thought by the Irish humans that they guard treasure hidden by the Vikings who first invaded the island." Ross said he had found no evidence of that theory, and Nell agreed with him.

What Ross hadn't been able to understand, no matter how hard he tried, was that leprechaun cobblers always make only one shoe, never two, so anyone needing a pair has to find another leprechaun to make the mate for it. Certainly if the leprechauns are actually all male, that didn't help Ross much in his search for a wife.

Ross had heard tales about another kind of Norwegian little people, the *nissen*. They were said to have settled on the farms around Dublin and demonstrated a special affinity for farm animals. Perhaps one day he could find a wife after all if he could to connect with the *nissen*.

Nell told him that the *nissen* 'little people' had probably arrived at various times aboard Norwegian-registered ships docking in Dublin Harbor. Pronounced niss'a, many of their descendents live in the outlying districts of Dublin. We had shared a few songs with some of them only the night before.

With that information, Ross brightened and seemed to look forward to his evenings with us.

Several days into our time together in Dublin, I asked Nell to tell me a bit more about her own history. Nell said that it is well recognized that Vikings explorers established the first permanent settlement in Dublin. She told me that her grandmother would speak longingly of the story passed down to her about our Norwegian ancestors.

"Grandma's distant ancestor was aboard one of the Viking ships that sailed up the River Liffey and overcame the Irish tribesmen defending the fort. I'm sure you've heard about that nasty battle that left the local population depleted and weary of the siege.

"These early Norse sailors were relieved to have created a place, at least for a time, where they could safely come ashore. As could be expected of those long ago days at sea, conditions on board had been less than ideal, populated as the ship was with rats and mice that had climbed aboard while the ship was being provisioned in Christiansand."

Continuing in the best tradition of Irish storytelling and longing for 'the old country,' Nell's granny told her that along with the unpopular rodents that fed on ship's supplies, had been another variety of stowaway. Her male ancestor of many generations past was called Oddvar, a curious looking little Norwegian troll. He came from a strain of trolls who were all much smaller than the usual bulky Norwegian species. His family home was a deep cave on the side of the berg that gave the Forberg farm its name.

"Because Oddvar was so tiny beside even the younger children in his family, and certainly minute compared to the other trolls in his school, Oddvar had been teased and ridiculed constantly his whole life, by absolutely everyone. To make things worse, Oddvar had always been a gentle being, given to help out wherever he could and unwilling to fight back, regardless the taunts.

"Perhaps that's why his children—and their children on down until you come to me—seem to have more of the caregiver, helper characteristics. I like best helping out little children at school," she told me.

"As they came into their teen years, Oddvar's younger brothers grew uglier by the day. Long hair, huge wild eyes, crooked noses, and sturdy but unfortunately bowed legs. They had taken to stealing cattle from adjacent farms and moving them onto the Forberg lands where they could become part of the resident herd and thus available whenever the troll family needed meat. At least none of Oddvar's people ate human flesh, as some trolls did. Cattle rustling was a practice of which he disapproved, and Oddvar resolved to find a way to somehow detach himself from his disreputable family. He wanted to learn to be a good doctor and assist in small ways any of the sleeping humans around him. The usual lifestyle of most malicious trolls was definitely not for him.

"Venturing forth to the farmhouse after dark one night and alone, Oddvar overheard the farmer's son, young Olav Forberg, telling his friends about the adventure he was about to undertake. He would be leaving on a sailing ship that would take him away from the dreary farm life and his deeply religious family, possibly forever. Olav told them that he had only this one evening for goodbyes because he had arranged to be picked up in the morning and taken to the docks.

"Oddvar made a very quick decision then. He returned home, grabbed his gear, and simply left."

Each time Nell's granny told the story, Nell tried to imagine what it would feel like to leave behind everything she had ever known. Ireland had always been her home and Norway had been his only home until then. Considering my recent arrival in a new country I could sympathize with Oddvar, and I told Nell so.

"Back at the Forberg farmstead, Oddvar rolled himself into the elder Forberg son's rain cape, a garment that he knew Olav wouldn't need until after the ship had sailed. By then, the travelling troll would be on his way to a new adventure and regardless of what came next—even being caught by humans in daylight and turned to stone—would be a better fate than this impossible life where he was always the different one."

So here was Nell with all the other 'little people' around her as she finished the story of her ancestor's departure from Norway. We were amazed that the details of Oddvar's leaving Norway and arrival in Ireland had been passed down through the generations. "Not a problem," said Nell. "The Norwegian trolls have always been good record keepers. Like human Norwegians, genealogy and our history is important so we always know the farm we came from and who our cousins are. Besides, all the Irish residents are great storytellers, so it has been a fine partnership."

"Now what is your best advice for me in finding a wife?" Ross asked the rest of us.

"Well as far as I know a nissen is much like an elf or gnome and they existed long before the time of Christ, so this ongoing conflict in Ireland between the Roman Catholic and the Protestant faiths is of no concern to them," offered one of our 'little friends.'

"That should make one of them a good choice for you."

"They are short and stocky, not unlike Nell's original ancestor," said another. "They wear clothing of wool, often red in colour, and usually a knitted red pointed hat. I've heard they are good to children, but I know they are especially kind to animals in the barn or stable of the family to which they attach themselves. You wouldn't mind living on a farm out in the country would you, Ross?"

"Of course not," was his reply.

"One thing you should know, Ross, is that nissen are fond of playing tricks, not unlike the brownie's test for a worthy family. I heard one time about a *nis* who moved the animals around in the barn, braided the horse's mane and tail, and stole hay from the cows to give to her favourite horse. This *nis* enjoyed helping horses more than cows, it seemed."

"The other part of the nissen character that humans must be wary of is that they expect respect. If *nissen* are not treated well, their trickery can extend to turning milk sour, causing sickness of both animals and people or even a crop failure. Their powers are not to be discounted. That is why on every farm a large bowl of sour cream porridge with a generous dollop of butter is frequently left out for them, and certainly every Christmas Eve. In Norway on Christmas Eve, a *nis* is chosen to deliver packages to the door where there are good children," concluded one of the older trolls.

With all of this encouraging news, Ross became visibly cheered and called the bartender to serve a round of drinks to everyone. There were toasts and speeches in celebration of the gathering of 'little people.'

With the coming of dawn and just as our party was about to break up, Nell climbed up on an old oak table and stomped her tiny feet to gain our attention.

"I have a great idea, she asserted. "Let's each one of us write a story about how we came to be in Dublin together for this multi-ethnic celebration. We can tell about the experiences of our forefathers in the place they came from, how and why they left, and what their life has become since leaving. Let's make it accurate but try to be interesting. That way we can leave a permanent record of all of our histories for those who come after us."

I know I had a huge scheming grin on my face when I replied, "You remember I told you that I have a special relationship with Somer Tullius, John's daughter. I've watched over her since she was a baby and she always had a winning way with her dad. I think there is a good chance, if I ask her, that she can convince John to publish our stories as a companion volume to the Maui Writers' book. We could call it *Little Friends in Ireland*. Now let's all get some rest and after dark tomorrow evening we can go looking on the farms around here for a female *nis* partner for Ross."

There once was a singer named Jerry,
Who took too much drink down in Kerry.
His limericks fell short,
They took him to court,
And sent him away on a ferry.

—Debra Lynn

*While playing golf on that world famous course at Adare
Manor, Limerick, Ireland, designed by the great Robert Trent Jones,
Sr., I got to thinking about Ireland's brutal treatment by its em-
pire-building neighbor to the east, Merry Olde England, which for
centuries ravaged Ireland in the name of peace. And then Norman
Mailer's Why Are We in Vietnam came to mind, a book about how
the U.S. ravaged Vietnam in the name of democracy, a book that
neither mentions Vietnam itself nor even takes place there, but has
everything to do with it.*

*So, there I was on this elegant golf course, playing with three
upstanding American men who seemed formidable, spoke with
authority, and had high regard for themselves. As I played along
with them through heavy winds and rain, these thoughts of poor
ravaged Ireland and sad desecrated Vietnam turned to yet another
land lately despoiled by formidable, authoritarian, arrogant American men—quite like these fellows, in fact, as they hauled their
modern clubs across this ancient battlefield.*

WHY WE ARE IN BAGHDAD
by Christopher Keane

For those of you who don't want to read about food in
Ireland, you're in luck. For those of you who are not fans of
statistics—*in the last war 22,876 Dubliners died in foreign lands*—
rejoice. For those of you who are dead set against reading
about sheep in the meadow and cows in the corn, I've got no
picture worth a thousand words.

Ah, but for those of you who want to know what it's like
to play a game, in hurricane wind, on one of the great patches
of Mother Nature's skin, molded by the hands of man con-
spiring to alter her, with gorse as high as your butt and frustration as deep as your nightmares, come along.

"This game's not about looking for a ball, kid," said one
of my playing partners. "It's about finding a target and not
looking back. We'll take this course to its knees and move on
to the next."

I had just duck-hooked my drive into the gorse and went looking for it. Where'd they get that: *duck hook*? "The curve of the duck's neck," another of them said, "Let's move on."

"What's the hurry!" I shouted above the wind.

They stopped. Their heads snapped around. They glared at me.

The people they stick you with on the first tee. There ought to be a screening process. Where else do you get stuck with strangers, for hours and hours, pressed together against your will? Elevators.

Their names were Geoff, DonLee and Dixon. They looked like CEOs or high-end government workers, in loud pro shop clothes you'd never be caught dead in anywhere but here.

Golf. What an odd game. Look who plays it. Not a team sport. You can play in a group but everybody's for himself. Proactive, not reactive. You live and die by your own decisions. *You* move the ball forward. No linemen, no shortstop to bail you out. You can play alone, and I, more often than not, prefer to.

I would have preferred it this day, what with these three jokers charging forward, looking at their watches every ten seconds. With no apparent strategy, they beat the ball until it submitted four, six, ten shots later, when they buried it in a hole in the ground.

"I don't want you standing on the green when I putt," Geoff said. Geoff had steel gray hair and a smirk you just want to slap right off his face. And he mumbled, as if mashed potatoes filled his mouth.

"What?" I said.

"Geoff has a problem with strangers getting too close at critical moments," Dixon said. "Humor him."

I waited by the bunker while he three-putted.

"If I'd been on the green my weight might have helped your ball to drop in," I said.

"Did you hear that, guys?" said Geoff. "We got a co-median with us."

Har har har.

I spotted DonLee, with his silver-gray Superman hair and

sweat-stained horn rims, over in the rough, pretending to look for his ball when there it was in front of him. He was punching it forward with the toe of his shoe until—look at that—it sat up pretty. This was not the first time DonLee would pull this stunt, nor the last.

Dixon sidled up alongside me. "Don't let it get to you," he said, letting me know that he knew that I saw DonLee, "He's under a lot of pressure and you should be able to enjoy yourself. If you have to bend the rules to get a pat on the back for a job well done, bend them. Have fun."

As DonLee said about a hundred times that day, "It's just a game, kid."

Dixon put his arm around me as a grandfather would. If Dixon weighed another eighty pounds and his neck were stuffed into his shoulders another inch or two, he'd be Jabba the Hutt. "I've been around a long time," he said, "and these boys like to pull a little wool every so often. Hell, we all do. You know what I mean."

"Cheating, and lying about it?"

"What, are you up for sainthood, kid? Let's move on."

Pernicious cloudbanks, packed tight with rain, swept off the Atlantic. We clumped down number 12, 435-yard par 4, dogleg right. On the green, Geoff, who was acting as if he were in charge of the day and night, missed a two-foot putt. He let rip a dozen expletives and rammed his putter head into the green, carving out a grave-like chunk of dirt.

DonLee filled in the hole and Dixon picked up the ball and the two of them followed Geoff to the 13th tee. I could have stuffed a sock in his mouth and tied him to a tree.

The harder Geoff tried, the worse he got, and the more belligerent and petulant he became. His unhappiness had no governor. He beat the ball, he tore up the greens, he emptied the traps.

On the 15th tee, Dixon followed Geoff into the men's room of a small, hut-like structure. A moment later they emerged, calm as flight. Geoff proceeded to launch a 260-yard drive straight down the middle. He even told a joke.

As I walked up the fairway toward my ball, DonLee the

Cheater appeared at my shoulder. "He's got a temper," he explained. "It's in the genes. His family tries to hide it. Don't let it bother you. He's still in the parental box, lived there all his life, so to speak. You know."

"No," I said, "I don't know."

"It doesn't matter. What matters is that Dixon has his Valium."

On the sixteenth green, Geoff dropped a four-foot putt. By the way he strutted about, with his arms pumping above his head, you'd think he sank the Navy.

"That's how you do it!" he shouted. "That's how it's done! How do you do it? Like that! You don't win by doing it *not* like that!"

"What does Geoff do?" I asked DonLee.

"Something crucial. We'll leave it at that."

At eighteen, Geoff hit a ball into the lake, and then another. And then he hurled his club after them, and then another. He ran to the lake's curtain where he crouched down, head between his knees, and cried.

This was no ordinary cry bursting through Geoff's pinched oscillating lips. This was the cry of someone severely disturbed. Finally, after a long pause, he stood up and gave his two clubs, now fast asleep on the lake's bottom, his benediction. "They deserved it," he said.

In the clubhouse after the round, we sat on the veranda overlooking the 18th green. Geoff, lifting his eyes from the scorecard, said at me, "You beat me."

"How could I beat you," I said, "when I wasn't playing against you?"

"You beat me and you know it."

Here was one of those moments you hate to live through because you know you're going to screw it up, but love to replay later in your head because you know you're going to win. Was Geoff picking a fight? I could see on his vinegary face the kind of tart little prick of a kid he used to be.

"Another orangeade?" Dixon said to me.

"He doesn't want another orangeade," said Geoff. "He wants to go."

I shuffled a deck of one-liners, decided to pass.

"Excuse me while I go the men's room," I said.

"That your style, tiger?" Geoff said, "Cut and run?"

"Or I could stay right here and evacuate all over you." Blood gorged my brain. "Then again," I said to his pig eyes, "you might like that too much. *Geoffy*."

In the parking lot, Dixon thanked me for the game and told me that he, DonLee and Geoff were heading east—*way* east, as he put it—to see how things were going at the first tee.

"The first tee?" I said.

"A piece of property we've been developing over there," said Dixon. "You know, kid, you have to start somewhere." He winked at me. "Remember, it's only a game."

I've always loved to travel, and have visited the UK several times, but the time in Ireland with the Maui group helped me see travel and exploration in a whole new way. The inspiration for Declan and Cailte and their transaction came from observing folks in Kilkenny and Cashel. A grumpy old man walking in the rain in Kilkenny caught my eye and his image stayed with me for several days. Another older man, cheerful and dapper, seemed to enjoy greeting tour buses and tried to get our driver to honk his horn. A poster advertising a search for a missing man in Cashel seemed to be the final element that brought the first two men together for me. The idea seemed much bigger than a short story, but the meeting of two such characters, and potential business dealings, presented an irresistible challenge.

THE TRAVELER'S WILES

by Margaret Stratton, Psy.D.

Declan walked down the muddy sidewalk, barely noticing the globs of mud sticking to his pants cuffs. The early evening breeze was soft and cool, but it blew cold in his soul, giving him no comfort. Dec turned into the door of The Traveler's Wiles, where he sensed he would find the chip he was bargaining for. He walked into the little pub and recognized many of those seated at the small tables, and nodded greetings to one or two he spied in the crowd. A dark wooden bar ran the length of the back of the room, its surface shiny from layers of varnish and years of polishing. Intricate carvings covered the base of the bar, figures in various scenes of frolic or mayhem. It didn't always pay to look too closely at those scenes. Occasionally one of the figures might turn and look back. If their scene were one of frolic they would simply wink or nod. But if they were carved into a setting of mayhem, the viewer might see a face twisted in terror, or worse, a glance that threatened to thrall and entrap. Even here, in a doorway to what was, there were beings that struggled to exert an evil influence.

One face in the carvings caught Declan's eye. The man carved there turned and looked him square in the eye, winked and nodded. The face seemed familiar and gave Dec a modicum of hope that his searchings had ended.

Declan ordered a half pint, and turned to find a place to settle down and wait. All the tables were full save one, where a thin, dapper older man sat. The dapper man had the same face as the carving that greeted Dec. After watching the man briefly, Declan approached him.

"Is this seat taken?" He asked.

"Not at all, friend, not at all. Be seated and be welcomed." The man smiled cheerily. "How do you find our little refuge from the cold night?"

"It's a cheery place, but it has some interesting wood work; I've never seen its like before," Declan replied.

"Ah, yes, our carvings. They do tell a story, don't they? Mind you, some say they don't bear looking at directly, but if you're not the superstitious kind, I'm sure you might enjoy the tales they could tell." The man's eyes sparkled with humor. "Many travelers come here just for those carvings. Some come to see the carvings, and some come to watch those who see them. Myself, I just enjoy the atmosphere of a real local pub, carvings or no."

"So you're not from around here?" Declan asked.

"Well, you see, man, I'm from here and from there, no real special place I'd want to call home. Where my hat is, is home, ya see." The man took a long drink of his dark beer. "And where do you call home?"

Declan paused, but so slightly that some might not have noticed. "I wander about, too. Left home so long ago, and I've seen so many things, I'd have to agree with you that where I hang my hat is my home for that day."

"Ah, a man after my own heart. I'm Cailte, by the way. Pleased to meet you." Cailte extended his hand.

"Declan, glad to meet you." He took Cailte's hand, which was cool, and surprisingly soft. "Let me buy you another pint."

"Thank ya, then, I wouldn't say no to another bit of

drink." Cailte polished off the dregs of his beer and handed the glass to Declan.

As Declan approached the bar, he could feel Cailte's eyes on him, sizing him up. He ordered two more pints and as the barkeep handed them over he nodded faintly to Declan. Declan responded as faintly. He returned through the crowded pub to Cailte's table.

"Here we go, and here's to new friends in new places." Declan raised his glass.

"I'll drink to that. To new friends, new vistas, and new ventures." Cailte tapped his glass on Declan's and took a deep drink. "So you're a traveler, like me. What brings you to this area?"

"I'm in the area looking for things that have been lost. That's my business, you see, lost things. So much history in the area, it's a fine business to be in." Declan said.

"Is that so, is that so? As it happens I know many who deal with those sorts of things, from different angles." Cailte's gaze sharpened. "Maybe that our interests could meet, so to speak. Do you contract your services to others?"

"No, no, I mostly work on my own, and serve my own interests. More profit that way, and it cuts out any middlemen. The fewer involved the better, I always say." Declan settled back into his chair. This was feeling more and more hopeful, yet he still needed to proceed carefully.

"Yes, it *is* good to cut out those who would drain off our profits, isn't it? Mind you, I do have an employer, so to speak, but he gives me free reign, within limits. Couldn't stand it if there was too much oversight. I am a man who enjoys my freedom, after all." Cailte chuckled. "My employer is an exacting man, but once his workers prove their mettle he lets them be, right enough."

"So what does your employer seek, that he sends you roving to find?" Declan asked.

"Well, now that's a tale, best told for another time. Suffice it to say, I find things that will contribute to my employer's future interests." Cailte took another drink and wiped some foam from his lips. "And what about you? You work for no man, and you seek lost things?"

"I look for things that might have been misplaced over time, overlooked, missed by few. I work in restoration, if you will." Declan felt as if he was edging toward a precipice, yet he needed to know if Cailte was indeed the one he sought.

"How interesting, how interesting. I just happen to know of some things that have been misplaced, and could perhaps put you in touch with those who could aid you in your searchings. Mind you, the price is a bit steep, but results are almost guaranteed." Cailte sat forward in his chair, his gaze sharper than ever.

"I would be interested, and I'm sure the price could be negotiated. Most things are negotiable these days." Declan pulled his chair closer to the small table. "I'm searching for a particular thing that went missing last month over in County Tipperary. Not something missed by many, but it had tremendous sentimental value for the family involved."

"Ah, County Tipperary, I was just there a few weeks back. A charming place. I happened to stop for a night in Cashel, do you know it?" Cailte pulled his chair closer to Declan and leaned in.

"Cashel, yes, I was there for a few days. Had to stop off and see some folks briefly. Not much there as I recall, just some ruins and tourist shops." Declan felt icily calm as he watched Cailte. Was this the traveler he'd heard of from Maisie?

"Yes, tourist shops, such fertile ground for, shall we say, expeditions for future business? So much goes on that things can easily get lost." Cailte settled back. He appeared to be enjoying the conversation.

"I'm searching for a particular thing that got lost, a sort of living thing, if you will." Declan mirrored Cailte's posture, relaxing back into his chair.

Cailte's eyes sharpened. "Ah, one who seeks living things lost. How intriguing. I'm thinking maybe I'm one who could help you. As it happens, living things lost are my specialty."

"How fortunate for me, then, to run into you." Declan took another drink.

"Yes, how fortunate. Let me see, from my inventory I recall only a few living things lost from Cashel. Would you have a particular one in mind?" Cailte seemed perfectly relaxed, but Declan could sense a tension in him.

"There was a simple man, a carver, who went for a walk through the countryside. His wife expected him back for supper and he never returned. His dog, Jake, returned at dark, but there's been no sign of the man since," Declan said.

"And of course the Gardá have been consulted?" Cailte said.

"Yes, but it was weeks ago and they've long since moved onto other matters. A simple man, missing this long, no one really seemed interested."

Cailte sat forward. "Good, all the better. These things get muddled when the local authorities get involved. I'm sure I could retrieve what you're looking for. But tell me, what's your interest in a simple man who's gone missing from an afternoon walk? Surely there is little value in a simpleton carver."

"Yes, a simple carver would have little value to me, but he was my sister's husband. Strange, but there you are. I'd gotten so tired of my rovings that I'd decided to give up the life. But how do you say no to an only sister?" Declan said.

Something shifted in Cailte's eyes. "Your sister's husband, you say. Unfortunate for her, and for you. With my employer, surrendering lost things to one who has an emotional attachment comes at a higher price. Are you sure it would be worth it?"

Declan sighed. "As I said, he is my only sister's husband, and I'd thought to make this my last recovery venture. I'd have to hear the price to decide if it's worth it."

"I'd say the price is seldom worth the trade, but then, you see, I'm a man who knows where my own interests lie. Attachments were always too messy for me, and not worth the effort to maintain. But then I am one of a rare sort, who can be content with what I draw from my work."

"So then, the price, Cailte. What would your, um, employer want for the man?" Declan asked.

"I'd say that in this case an even trade would suffice, your life for his. Fair to my employer, I get a bit of a boost as you're clearly not simple, and your sister gets her carver back." Cailte watched Declan closely.

Declan looked hard at Cailte. "Is this the standard 'deal' your employer offers?"

Cailte chuckled. "No, I do have a bit of freedom in how I make my deals. He leaves it to me how I maintain my 'inventory,' so to speak. But mind you, once a deal's made, it is firm; no going back."

"I mentioned negotiations. You want a life for a life. How about a lesser life, say one that is on its way out, for the life of my brother-in-law." Declan offered.

"No, no, I don't think so. We have, indeed, acquired some who were already on the way out, but there's much less fun in that, and much less for me to gain from personally. I think I'll stick to the bargain I offered. Take it or leave it." Cailte grinned.

Declan hesitated.

"Take your time." Cailte offered. "I'm in no hurry. But you might want to know that the carver might be out of reach if we don't make a deal tonight."

Declan had grown weary of his life, of the tasks he'd been given to do. He felt broken and soiled to his soul, and had hoped that this small act of helping his sister might offer him a modicum of cleansing. But was he prepared to go this far, for a brother-in-law he barely knew? Perhaps, on the other hand, there was another way unseen by Cailte.

"I guess you leave me no choice," he said. "I'm prepared to accept your offer, but the transaction must take place on my terms. I am, after all, the one with the most to lose."

"And what might the terms be, then? I can't be too careful in these matters, you understand."

Declan said, "The transaction takes place here, tonight. You're able to bring the carver here, correct? And what guarantee do I have that after the trade is made you'll release him?"

Cailte grinned. "Well, now, that's the problem, isn't it? I

am, after all, a business

man and collector. What sorts of guarantees would you want?"

Declan reached into his jacket pocket and pulled out a piece of paper and a pen. "Let's write a brief contract, which you'll sign. I'll give this to the barman to witness and instruct him to deliver it to the Gardá in Cashel. You likely work best when you can move about undetected, and the involvement of the Gardá would certainly hinder your work, in Cashel at least. It would be important for you to keep markets open for yourself, correct?"

Cailte laughed. "You are a canny man. Of course I don't want undue attention from the Gardá, and Cashel has been a great site for collection activities. I could always abandon the area for a while, but I've grown comfortable here. Perhaps a weakness I've developed in my advancing years. Yet I see the sense of your offer, and I can grant you that small concession."

Declan went to the bar and spoke quietly to the barman. The barman looked over at Cailte and back at Declan and nodded. Declan returned through the crowd to the small table and sat down. He wrote briefly on the scrap of paper and handed it over to Cailte.

"I, Declan O'Rourke, determine to trade my soul for that of the carver, Mattie O'Brien. This trade will be final, and will remove any claim made by those who had made such claim on Mattie or those related by marriage or blood to Mattie."

Cailte nodded at the wording. "You've made it clear I'm to leave the carver, and his family, alone. Clever, that. Ok, we have a deal. Shall we shake on it and share a final pint?"

"Let's just shake and get the transaction done. I'll sign and then you can sign below my name, and I'll hand it to the barkeep." Declan's voice was firm.

"Have it your way, my man. I have to say, you're very matter-of-fact for facing such a major transaction. Wish I had your savoir faire, but I am, after all, one who is committed to self-preservation," Cailte said. He extended his hand and shook Declan's. "Maybe if we'd met in different circumstances we might have worked well together. Might even have gone into business together and done my employer out of business. Ah, well, no use wishing for what won't happen, right?"

Declan signed the paper and pushed it across the little table. "Here you go, sign it yourself. Here, use my pen. I don't want any disappearing ink. You are a canny businessman, after all, and I'd guess that you've done many transactions in your time."

Cailte roared with laughter. "There's just no fooling you, is there, man? However, I no more trust your writing instrument than you do mine. See if our barman has a spare pen, and we'll sign the bargain." Still laughing to himself, Cailte watched as Declan approached the barman. The tavern keeper looked at him, then at Cailte, and shrugged his shoulders. He offered Dec a tray with several pens of various sorts on it: a fancy quill pen with a sharp nib, a pen carved out of oak, one that appeared to be made of ivory, and a crude bone pen.

Declan returned to the table and placed the tray in front of Cailte.

"Ok, now you have your choice of writing instruments, untouched by me. Sign away and let's get this over with."

Cailte grabbed the solid oak pen, examined its tip, and began to write. As he began to sign his name, the pen, and his hand, began to glow bright red. He looked up, frightened, and shouted, "What.....?" But before he could get more out, the red glow moved rapidly up his arm and in a flash covered his whole body. His eyes opened wide in terror and he shrieked soundlessly in understanding.

A brief flash, a soft puff of air, and his chair was filled with dark ash.

A few patrons nearby looked over, clearly startled. One look on Declan's face and they quickly turned and huddled back into their own groups.

Declan brushed bits of ash from his jacket and pulled the contract back across the table. "A life for a life, he said. Well, that's done then."

He sat very still for a moment, eyes closed in deep concentration. He murmured a few soft words, and gestured to the chair across from him. A short, middle-aged man appeared in the chair and looked around with confusion.

"Declan, where am I? What are you doing here?"

Declan smiled gently. "You're okay, Mattie, you just got lost on your walk, do you remember? I found you here in County Limerick and we decided to stop here for the night. I'll get you back to Cashel in the morning."

"Funny, Dec, I don't seem to remember that. I did meet a man who offered me a meal and a drink, cause you know, I'd wandered too far to get home by supper. Is Lara too worried? I couldn't find Jake, either. It got dark after I had my supper with the man, and then I can't remember what happened. I do hope Jake is okay, and my Lara isn't upset. Let's go home tonight, Dec. I feel awful tired and I want my own bed."

"Ok, Mattie. We'll go home." Declan stood with Mattie and turned to leave the pub. As he passed the barman he paused. "Tell the boss I finished the job. One less collector to bother the locals. But tell him we have to discuss my contract. I'm thinking I want to get out of the business. Retrievals are getting harder and I'm just feeling too old for the job."

The barman looked at him hard. "Nobody gets out of this business alive, Dec, and nobody knows that better than you. I'll send word on up, and we'll see what we can do. See you soon."

Dec sighed. "I'm out, man, no matter what it takes. I'll be the first to get out alive, mark my words." He leaned on the bar, shoving aside half-empty pint glasses, and tapped three times, softly, on the shiny bar surface. A shudder ran through the wooden carvings, halting their frolic and mayhem, and if one had ears to hear, a shriek rose from them in unison.

The barkeep shook himself, as if waking from a daydream. "Well man, are you going to have another pint or not? I don't have all evening."

"No, man, thanks, but I have places to go and things to

do. I'll settle the account when next I'm here."

Declan turned and walked out into the cold night air.

From a quiet street bounded by ancient wall, we walked through the old city gate, around a stone chapel, dropping into a park surrounded by traffic noise. I saw a little girl with curly blond hair throwing a ball. Her father watched over her. It isn't so much that I wondered about their story, but the juxtaposition of the peace of the garden and intensity of the traffic gave me a story of a man who tried to seem confident and not show his wife and daughter the terrible emotion that raged in him.

FAITH AND HOPE
by Heather Varez

On two sides of the chapel garden, traffic sped by with its growls and moans, creating a terrifying obstacle. Lloyd watched Chloe with a diligence that was not usually required of him. It was Mary, his wife, who guarded Chloe. It was she who would smile every time the girl turned and grinned with joy.

On another side of the garden was an ancient wall, built to defend against, at worst, a trebuchet. Towering over father and daughter, was a church, built even before the wall.

He glanced at the church door. Tall enough to egress giants. Tension raced up his spine, taking his shoulders closer to his ears.

He turned back to see Chloe throw the ball as high as she could. The ball arched and fell to the pavement with a faint splat. It neither bounced nor rolled very far. That too was Mary's idea. No chance of Chloe chasing it into some danger.

Lloyd glanced again at the door. He was waiting while inside, his wife joined the dead of eight hundred years requesting life. Not all of the dead rested in the chapel, of course. Only the rich were encased in the stone of the vault.

Splat went the ball and Chloe hopped down three steps to catch it. Her smile was as bright as the little daisies that created snowy patches in the grass. As healthy as the constructed riot of color set in a line behind him. Red, yellow, purple and pale pink were brushstrokes of vitality against aged walls.

They would wilt and die before the year ended.

Inside the church, his sweet Mary prayed among all the formerly wealthy who wished immortality. They had tried to find longevity in stone statues and brass placards. In the end, nobody remembered them and few cared who they were. Each of them lived their blink of a life, and the trail of remembrance faded soon away, as even those left behind died.

There was no stopping death, but the unconcerned three-year-old threw her ball and chased after it among the color and road noise.

Lloyd scraped his foot along the cobbled stones. His chest burned with the desire to yell. To cry out his frustration. He could only watch his daughter play on the stairs that ended in the racing blips of speeding cars.

The doors creaked open but he would not turn. He couldn't look at this woman, not yet. Her hand, pale and gentle, touched his shoulder and he turned, pulling her into his embrace, putting his chin on her head. So small, and with hair only a little darker than Chloe's pale curls, she cuddled into him. He knew that if he looked at her face, he wouldn't be able to hold back the roiling emotion he had so carefully dammed. He ignored the pregnant bulk of her belly.

Chloe ran to them, grinning and ready for the family hug they had done so often. When they didn't pick her up immediately, she frowned and pulled at her mother's arm. Lloyd tried to swallow the lump that nested in his throat. As one, the adults each grasped one of the tiny uplifted hands and Chloe was levitated into their embrace.

In her world all was well.

Faith had deserted Lloyd, but faith was intrinsic to Mary. After all, she was the namesake of the most holy of mothers. To him, all mothers had some aspect of the holy. Once Mary became a mother, all those around became her children. When Chloe was born, Mary began to lay out his clothes. He enjoyed that special treatment, but as Chloe grew she began to speak to baby talk, all the time.

Though the Holy Mother cared for all, even she had her favorites. It was the fragile and dependant who must be cared for first.

It was Mary's job to care for the children. This one who had her tiny arms thrown over her parents' shoulders, and...

He set Chloe down and turned to the gate, trying not to squeeze Mary's hand. The time of judgment had come.

Three stories up, sitting in a miasma of sickness, disinfectant, and imagined death, Lloyd watched the clock tick off interminable hours.

Mary had gone through the cold metal doors into the unknown, leaving him alone again. When Mary had left, Chloe placed her hands on his knees and smiled. He leaned down and she threw her arms around his neck. "It's alright, daddy." She kissed his cheek.

Now she lay across the molded plastic seats with his jacket covering her. His little finger twitched. Up and down, it thumped on his jeans. He bit one side of his bottom lip and stopped it with conscious effort for the hundredth time.

Two nurses came out of the same doors Mary had gone through. The door sounded like a gunshot to him and he jumped.

Both women were smiling narrow smiles. Did that mean the thumb was up or had some evil audience cheered death into pointing thumb toward earth?

"Mr. Dannery, I'll sit with Chloe. Why don't you go in and see your wife?"

Restraint cracked just enough for a shaky smile. His wife was alive. He wanted to know no more than that. His sweet waited for him.

He left Chloe to pass through the doors contemplated for too long.

Mary lay upright on several pillows, only a shade or two darker than the sheets. Her smile, however, was as warm as whiskey and it began to thaw him. He walked up and took her hand.

"The babies are both boys. They took them away as soon as they came out. I don't know how they are. The nurses won't say anything."

Rory and William. Those were the boys' names they had chosen. That was back before they found out that one was stealing from t'other. The doctors decided to take both before they died, but at thirty weeks, they shouldn't make book on survival.

Another nurse came in. She wanted to take them to the nursery.

"How are they?" Mary asked

She smiled but it was a plastic smile, meant to pacify. "The doctor will speak to you soon. I'll take you, Mrs. Dannery. Nurse Pikford will take you to get dressed, Mr. Dannery."

Dressed? Did he need a jacket to meet the doctor? The doctor who would tell him all bets were off?

Mary's departure left a vacuum. Sound was sucked from his ears even as his vision narrowed for a moment. It cleared just in time for the nurse to stick her head in to see him still standing.

She smiled. "Come, Mr. Dannery."

He didn't want to. Every bit of him wanted to run. The kindness in her eyes cursed him for the coward he was. Heart beating a heavy metal rhythm, he followed the nurse, into the unknown and undesired. She led him into a room and handed him blue pants, smock and booties. The pressure returned to just behind his eyes as he was led to the sink that jutted out on one side. She ordered him to wash his hands with astringent-smelling orangish goo.

It wasn't too late. He could turn around right now and run out those doors. He could grab beautiful Chloe, healthy Chloe, and just run.

His body moved instead to the opposite door as he followed the nurse. One more set of frigid steel doors. A distorted reflection faced him. He thought it was probably his true self, horribly deformed in body as he was in mind. Reflections wouldn't lie. Then with an elbow to a big square button, the nurse opened the doors. He entered.

Mary sat in a rocking chair, utterly anachronistic in this setting of machines. Red and green lights flashed, monitors beeped and buzzed, and pumps breathed into tiny covered beds.

His eyes jerked from those machines back to Mary. She held something, a blue cocoon. Then a corner of the blanket twitched.

He was pulled forward by something, against his will until the tiny face was revealed. Its eyes were closed. *His* eyes were closed. Lloyd's fingers tingled.

He didn't know if this was Rory or William.

A tiny translucent hand escaped swaddling and curled against the blanket. Tiny lips sucked even as the plastic prong pushed air into little underdeveloped lungs.

"Mr. Dannery?" He turned to see the same nurse who led him in. She was holding another bundle. Something in him screamed but he ignored it. Without thought, he raised his arms to accept the bundle.

This was his son. Where before he had no hope, just the sight of the little struggling thing—baby—now hope built, swelled, and bubbled over. It covered him in warmth. He trembled and put his fingertip into the miniature hand. The baby grasped him in a soft grip.

Lloyd smiled at his tiny son.

A milkmaid from Castle Bunratty
—now I hope that you won't think I'm catty—
Kissed the tinker for pay,
Had a roll in the hay,
And emerged with a bun in her tatty.

—Judith Heath

The Rock of Cashel, ancient seat of the Kings of Munster, was a major religious center in the middle ages and is now an Irish Public Heritage monument. Five buildings and a cemetery, clustered high atop a limestone outcrop, create an atmosphere that is both sacred and spooky. The site provided an evocative setting for my allegory about a woman's spiritual journey at midlife. Her companion St. Michael the Archangel was well known to the early Irish monks. Prayers for intercession by St. Patrick and St. Michael, originally written in old Gaelic, are still offered around the world today.

HAWK'S WINGS

by Margaret Zacharias

The distinctive call of an Irish hunting hawk interrupted Megan Walsh where she stood near St. Patrick's cross, gazing down at monastery ruins from the curtain wall that encloses the Rock of Cashel. She turned to scan the crumbling cathedral rising on the hill to her right. She located the hawk's perch just as he launched himself from the top of an ancient round tower, with another resounding "kek-kek-kek."

As she looked back out over the Cashel valley, the hawk fluttered down to hover in the air only a few feet from where she stood. He waited right in front of her, flapping his wings and staring into her face as if he knew her. Just what she needed, Megan thought. A few of these birds had been known to attack human beings who had trespassed on their territory. She suddenly remembered that she was alone up here. The rest of her group had escaped the cold rain and walked into town for some dinner.

Megan backed away from the overlook, recalling the comfortable niches she had seen inside what remained of the cathedral. She sprinted up the stairs into its shelter, and crouched behind thick stone walls at the threshold while she made sure that the hawk had not followed her. Then she collapsed onto a boulder marking the center of the transept crossing.

No wonder, she thought, that ancient kings and church-men had erected these sturdy buildings, to conceal them-selves from the unpredictable forces of nature. She felt safer here, reassured to be inside the perimeter of stacked and mortared stones. Although the four original transepts had lost their coverings long ago, a vaulted roof still protected the central crossing from the rain.

The hawk appeared again. She could see him through the open east choir, circling high above her. Why had he ap-proached her at the curtain wall? Megan watched him per-form the acrobatic sky dance she had admired in another bird, above her Iowa home, at the end of winter. She had welcomed that first hawk's large stick nests in the wood-lands bordering her yard. She had known he would capture the pestilent rodents that gnawed on her tulips and lilies. He would frighten away the itinerant crows who stole gluttons' shares of her berries.

Then again, at the airport earlier this spring, she had spot-ted a similar hawk—it might even have been the same one—swooping into a field by the runway while she waited for her flight to depart. That hawk had come without warning, almost faster than her eye could follow. He flashed through the sky with the sun behind him, to capture his prey in his talons before he soared away.

Now here was another formidable hawk, and this one was frightening Megan. Perhaps in County Tipperary, she should address him by his Gaelic name: *"rí-seabhag."* The King Hawk's prowess as a hunter had endeared him to gen-erations of royalty. But even at an ancient Irish castle, Megan thought, *this* raptor should not be appearing *this* often. She was feeling pursued, and a little bit provoked.

Cooper's hawks flew reconnaissance in Iowa; sparrow hawks nested in Ireland. Those were what she expected to see when she encountered a hawk. Yet these rare King Hawks were starting to be as populous in the air as the white-tailed deer were on the ground.

The aggressive hawk seemed to have disappeared for the

moment. Megan had decided she was calm enough to walk down the hill and rejoin her group, when she began to hear faint music. The sounds of flutes and fiddles were rising through the patter of the rainstorm. As she listened, the melody grew louder. Megan recognized the strains of "Danny Boy." But who were these musicians, and where were their instruments?

One by one, then two by two, and then in a swarming mass, the gargoyle figures carved on the corbels, capitals and lintels suddenly sprang to life. The gargoyles danced on the transept walls, swung down on ropes from the lancet windows, and somersaulted through the quatrefoils. Megan was terrified.

These hideous creatures apparently inhabited every nook and cranny where she had hoped to hide from the hawk. As she tried to determine how she could escape them, a female figure the tour guide had called a *sheela-na-gig* broke away from the wall, and sauntered up to Megan.

"I can see you are tired," the *sheela-na-gig* said. "And you have done enough. Come with us, Megan Walsh, join the dance. We sleep all day; we feast and sing all night. Put your troubles behind and be lonely no more. Come away with us."

The *sheela-na-gig* spoke the truth, Megan thought. Her sons' educations and their two recent weddings had exhausted her. She should be happy to relax. Yet she had found herself feeling dismayed and bereft. She had run away to Ireland to examine her options, to try to decide how she wanted to spend the years that were left of her life.

Just as if they could read her thoughts, a chorus of gargoyles began to repeat the refrain. "Come away, come away, come away with us." Their dogged insistence in the clattering rain was unnerving. "No," Megan said, and shook her head.

Annoyed by her refusal, the creatures surrounded her. They began to pinch, hurl rocks and pull Megan's hair. The *sheela-na-gig* turned haughty.

"You're an old woman, Megan, and your happiest years

are behind you," she said. The creatures grabbed hold of Megan and dragged her across the north transept floor. They pulled her out the door and into a graveyard that lay beyond the medieval round tower. "Come away, come away, come away with us, to the life of eternal frivolity. Dance and play, come away and labor no more."

"No," Megan said. "I still have work to accomplish."

"You are done," the *sheela-na-gig* said. "All that remains is sorrow and mourning. Escape with us and forget."

"Escape and forget," the chorus echoed. "Come away, come away and forget."

"My family still needs me," Megan insisted.

"They are gone," the *sheela-na-gig* said. "Your sons have wives, and jobs and lives. Those young folks hope they will never grow old. They hope they will never be slow and hollow like you."

"You lie!" Megan cried, as tears filled her eyes. She tried to shake the creatures away, but they clung like leeches to her skin.

With the whistling sound of a raptor's plunge, the King Hawk swept down from the top of the round tower and landed in the cemetery. The youngest creatures leaped on his back, thinking to have a ride, but he picked them out of his feathers with his beak as if they were insects. The wiser ones backed away, waiting to see what he would do. They were hoping for his imminent departure.

But the hawk remained like a courtier at Megan's feet, peering up into her face with intense concentration. She almost felt glad he had joined the group, as long as he stayed where he was. He, at least, revealed no fear of these unholy beings.

When the hawk did not immediately soar away, the hostile creatures resumed their pinching and pulling. They combined their strength to push Megan down, forcing her body into the soft ground. As she sank deeper and deeper into the peat, the hawk began to expand and change. He emerged in the form of a man. Astonished, Megan recognized her old friend Michael.

"You came back! You came back to help me. Stop them, Michael! They are trying to take me away."

"Alas, my fair Megan," Michael replied, "I cannot help you. *'Is geis dom é a dhéanamh.'* I am forbidden to do it. This *'gheasa'* was given before I was appointed to accompany you. Remember, I told you on the plane?"

When Michael had materialized in the seat next to her on the flight to Dublin, Megan had thought it fortunate that her archangel friend had showed up when he did. Otherwise, he would have landed on her head as she stretched out to sleep over the Atlantic Ocean. He had looked perfectly normal, the way he always did, wearing his favorite pea green Polo shirt and khaki slacks. He had not looked angelic at all.

But Megan had felt a familiar flicker of fear. He might not have come, as he had once or twice, to assist her in her mortal life. Perhaps this time her friend had been sent to retrieve and transport her soul. She knew that despite his ability to manifest himself as a mortal man, Michael was in fact a warrior archangel. He had defeated Lucifer's rebellion and would lead the last battle for heaven. Michael had always promised her that she would not die alone.

Megan's fears of imminent death had not been assuaged when five minutes later a blinding flash of lightning had struck the wing of the plane. She had felt the sizzle right through her bones, from the roots of her hair to the pads of her toes. But miraculously, the wing remained intact. This had not been the first time Michael had flown her safely through a storm. But Megan was still suspicious.

As soon as the turbulence had settled down she had asked him, "Michael, why are you here?"

His green eyes had been gleaming with leprechaun mischief. His hair had still been growing in that little thatch of ash blond wisps, around the bald spot at the top of his head. She had known he was planning to tease her.

"Shall I say it's because you've done a fine job of bringing up those boys? Could I convince you it's my reward for finishing my last mission? Or would you believe I've come to protect your search for a priceless treasure?"

"Would I argue instead you've been found overdue for some kissing at Blarney Castle?" Megan fell easily into their familiar rhythm. "Or maybe the truth is you've simply indulged in one Guinness pint too many?"

"I'm telling you the truth," Michael said, turning serious. "There *is* a treasure waiting for you, if you've enough courage to win it."

"Okay, Michael, what is this treasure?" Megan asked. "And where will I find it?"

"If I told you that, Megan—it would not be your own treasure then, now would it?"

"If I have to go search and find it myself, then why do I need you?"

"Why don't you rest and wait awhile, to see how useful I might be?"

"Yes," Megan thought, "I definitely need some sleep. This is too impossible altogether, probably hallucination, brought on by stress and severe sleep deprivation. I can't see why he'd appear to me now. I'm on vacation! When I wake up, he'll be gone." And just like that, she had dozed off.

By the time the plane had landed in Dublin, Megan had managed to convince herself that Michael's appearance had been only a symptom of jet lag. She hated long flights, strapped into a cramped economy seat. She had decided she was lucky to have suffered no more than a transient illusion, the result of wishful thinking.

"But what can I do?" Megan asked Michael now, from where she lay trapped in the peat by the gargoyles. "I'll never escape their evil chorus alone."

"Yet alone you must do it, if you mean to escape at all," Michael told her. "I'm not, however, forbidden by *'gheasa'* to give you a single clue."

"Oh yes, please do! Michael, help me—give me a clue?"

But he remained stoic and silent, refusing to move, as more and more creatures leapt in to pounce on Megan, and pummel her with sticks and rocks. She was becoming certain that she was overcome and would spend eternity in this muddy yard where the inscriptions on the gravestones bore witness to her ancestors.

Just before she disappeared altogether, she noticed that a small family of deer had quietly crept through the rain up the hillside. She spotted them peering in from the edge of the cemetery; they were watching her with what seemed like concern.

Yes! Megan remembered. She remembered Michael telling her how St. Patrick had once escaped his enemies by turning himself into a deer. With her last strength, she began to whisper St. Patrick's Breastplate, "*I arise today through the strength of heaven . . . light of the sun . . . swiftness of wind. . . depth of the sea . . . firmness of earth and . . . stable rock.*"

As Megan finished this incantation, the ground beneath her ceased giving way. The weight of the gargoyles could force her down no deeper. But the imps continued to beat her as she persevered, "*I arise today through God's strength to pilot me . . . God's might to uphold me. . . God's shield to protect me . . . God's host to preserve me from anyone wishing me ill.*" When Megan spoke these words, her strength returned. She was able to get to her knees, stand up and push away her attackers.

But the *sheela-na-gig* now opened a pouch that hung from a loop on her belt. She pulled out a tiny golden horn and blew three discordant notes. From every valley all around them, up the mountainside little creatures came running— *banshees* wailing, *gancanaghs* lusting, every unkind spirit seething—all of them summoned by the sound of the horn.

While Megan continued invoking the Breastplate, "*Christ defend me . . . Christ before me, Christ behind me. . . Christ beneath me, Christ above me . . .,*" Michael at last was freed to come forward. He laid his hands on her head. "*Rí-seabhag,*" he said, and Michael the man disappeared.

The King Hawk spread his wings, launching himself up and out of the graveyard. To Megan's astonishment, she discovered she also had wings! She sprang into the air and spread them, following his lead. As they caught the wind and rose, she could see the thwarted burial squadron stamping and raging far below them.

Michael and Megan flew in tandem, streaking through the clouds, rolling, diving, soaring and gliding on invisible currents. They flew over pastures thick with nourishing grass, hosting an embarrassment of fat glossy cattle. They soared above fluffy newborn lambs frolicking in gorse-bordered fields. They landed at last near the foot of the ancient Rock.

Megan stumbled as she came to her feet and Michael reappeared as a man. He steadied her with his hands. *"Geall dobhriste,"* he said. *"Tá grá imish agam dhuit."* He told her that she had indeed found her treasure: the sacred promise of God's unconditional love. Her life was changing and much she had depended on for meaning was now gone. But the important commitments still endured.

"Thank you, Michael," she whispered, as the King Hawk sailed away. He circled three times above the Rock; he dipped his wings to Megan once more before he turned west to the sea. She watched him go until he finally disappeared entirely. Then Megan Walsh composed her heart, and turned her feet towards home.

Sometimes the decisions that seem unjustifiable have been given the most thought and are provoked by the best of intentions. This piece is dedicated to a college roommate I hope found peace. If not, there were some of us who did understand.

DUBLIN TIME

by Bonnie Christoffersen

From the moment she woke that morning, she knew she would leave him, the thought, nothing new. But on this day, it resonated with truth.

"Maybe flowers," he was saying, already dressed and distracted, hurrying her along. "If you need to get out, maybe flowers. That, I think, would be a nice touch. Lots of greens. The flowers, white. For a five-star hotel, the room's terribly gold and brown, don't you think?"

"Flowers." She responded. "And I can use the time alone."

"But I thought you'd take Cameron with you. I kind of need you to take him, Annie. At least for a few hours."

"For flowers? Really, Josh. He's been a sport so far. But really. Flowers? Wouldn't it be better if he stayed with you?"

"You know I need the break. The quiet. I've hardly had a moment to think."

"But yesterday—"

"This could change my career. We've talked about this, Annie. The interview. It could change everything. Our lives."

She had not argued with him. Instead, that single thought crossed her mind as she took Cameron in hand (her son already dressed, this something Josh demanded. No breakfast until the clothes are on. The hair combed. A man of order—that was Josh. The kind of husband who color-coordinated his shirts with his ties in the closet. Socks to match). She thought. *Today I will leave him*. And in thinking this, she felt some guilt in nudging Cameron out the door.

They were in Dublin and, so far, she was enchanted by the city. Perhaps it was the pace that made it seem so alive. Pedestrians moved swiftly and everywhere, in hurried approaches and departures. But where were they headed? Was there some common destination? Or was the motivation from where they had come?

There was a rhythm to the crowds. Not so much a hustle but a determination that unified pedestrians in a single-minded assertiveness. Men, women, children—they flowed in a current. Similar to the beating of a heart, they caused the passing of time to seem urgent. Not that Annie was wearing a watch. Nor was there a clock—some landmark to hear chiming the hour. Like Big Ben. Wasn't that the way *Mrs. Dalloway* began?

Often, Annie thought in terms of the novel she once hoped to rewrite (how absurd to think this now), into something contemporary. What audacity! But then again, she was only in college, though youth is hardly license to imagine one capable of doing what *Apocalypse Now* did with *Heart of Darkness*. It was a dream. To think she could retell a story that could not be told better, but only differently. She, Annie, had even made a stab at it in college—a short story she thought later to expand into a novel. It received such praise from her professor. Peter. That was his name. Dr. Peter Yardell. And it was Peter, she seems to remember now, who was the suitor of Mrs. Dalloway in her younger years. Annie had made this man the redeemer of her alleged novel (never written). She had Peter orchestrate Mrs. Dalloway's escape from a life that, on the surface, seemed so frivolous. Of course she, Annie, was sleeping with that professor, her Peter, who praised her on so many levels. All this before the window incident. Then, he would have nothing to do with her.

Josh was different. He was a student, like herself, and had come to the hospital daily, imagining her to be some princess in a tower only someone like himself could truly save. He turned her life around. This is what everyone said. So, what need had she to write that novel? While now, there was no Big Ben to strike the hour. Yet, she was on a mission similar to that of Mrs. Dalloway in the opening pages written by Virginia Woolf. Mrs. Dalloway had been headed out to purchase flowers for a party. But Annie, unlike Mrs. Dalloway, was not alone. She was accompanied through the hustle and bustle of a Friday morning in Dublin with her six-year-old son, Cameron, who was so very quiet, holding her hand so tight it was almost painful.

"We can't cross here," she said to the boy. "But there. With the light."

The traffic surged past. She had to hold her son back.

"Oww, Mama," he said. "I wasn't going anywhere. I know to watch for the light." But he was looking the other way. Overhead in fact. "Is that a pigeon, Mama?" he asked and pointed to what flew pivoting in and out of the traffic.

"Yes. A pigeon," she said but winced to see how carelessly that bird maneuvered the air. So quick. Dipping just inches above the cars. Fool bird, she thought. But for that pigeon, *What a lark!*

She thought this again, the words repeated in her head. *What a lark.* This phrase was used so explicitly by Virginia Woolf to establish the character of Mrs. Dalloway. Words so light as to be weighted. *What a lark.* She, Annie, had used that phrase as well in a little piece she handed in to Peter Yardell, her professor. She had borrowed from Virginia's rhythm, stringing her phrases together so they rang lyrically. Swiftly. She too had felt the urgency. Especially when adding that other phrase of Virginia's. *What a plunge.* This, perhaps, leading to the incident with the window.

Of course, the window would never have beckoned if not for that earlier incident with the car. It was her injury, she thought now, that gave Josh the confidence to propose to her. After all, she had balanced more than one suitor before marrying Josh. Not so long after that, Cameron was born. This, after battling years of court appearances, preceded by a day that began as a lark and ended in catastrophe. Ten years ago now, that day that brought her forward to this—a Friday in Dublin when she knew she had no choice but to leave him.

"There were flowers at the arcade. Remember, Cam? You liked the arcade. Back where the fortuneteller was. Remember?" And already she regretted her suggestion.

Her son had wanted his palm read. This just yesterday (their very first day in Dublin). It had frightened her. His desire. He had made a scene, demanding what she resisted, this so unlike Cameron who by nature was such a quiet boy. So well behaved, his teachers said. But then again, how often had she refused him anything?

Rarely was she one to disagree, this the reason Josh tolerated those times she drank, becoming melancholy and sometimes, belligerent. Josh was always right (or so it seemed). Back when he promised to make her happy. Back when he suggested having a child might change everything. It was easiest to agree. Always and completely. Back when he thought he could save her. This after the incident with the window when it became painful for her to simply look in a mirror.

He told her she was beautiful even then. Perhaps this is why her body had healed with such success. A miracle, they said. No longer did she hide behind a curtain of hair, the jaw reconstructed, the nose realigned, not to mention having learned to walk again. And walk she did, and at an admirable pace. But this was unnecessary now. They had left the milling crowds, having stepped into the surprisingly empty arcade through an open gate of wrought iron. The arcade was closed, the vendors not yet arrived, their wares imprisoned, or perhaps, protected and safe, dismissed at night so lives could be lived and families maintained. And now, the hour too early. Even the fortuneteller was absent, her harem-like stall closed.

No flowers to be purchased here until later in the day.

"We'll go somewhere else. The other way," she said but she was looking in the mirror that hung above the fortuneteller's booth, surprised to see how right they looked together—mother and son. An attractive pair. She leaned to kiss Cameron lightly on the forehead.

"I love you Mommy," he said, but without conviction. He was remembering his disappointment of the day before, she thought. He was still angry that she refused him the reading of his palm.

"I know," she answered. "And I love you. Always."

They exited from the direction they had come. They traveled around the block and down the street to where she knew there would be flowers to purchase even at this early hour. And why? Because the morning really was quite beautiful. Too beautiful for the street vendors not to enjoy. "What a lark," she said, squeezing his hand, voicing what she repeated in her head.

Cameron looked up at her and frowned.

"It's an old expression," she assured him. "It means I'm enjoying your company very much."

He smiled and pointed further down the street. "There's a church, Mommy. A church with a red door. We should go inside. I want to open the red door."

They had visited cathedrals all of yesterday but none with red doors. Saint Patrick's. St. Theresa's. The Augustinian Church. She could not remember all the names and that seemed important now. Not that she was religious. She was not. Neither Anglican nor Catholic. But she had knelt at the altar in each of these churches and prayed. So it seemed awkward she could not remember the names. Or the colors of the doors. Never red. She was sure of this. Now, she had to help Cameron pull what he wanted to push. These doors were heavy for what appeared light in their brightness. Fire-engine red. Inside, the foyer opened to a chapel small and intimate.

"Look at the windows. They're beautiful." Cameron said.

"Yes. Beautiful," she replied.

"And they each tell a story." Someone spoke from behind her. A small man approached, his hands crossed in front of him, waist-high.

"We have to go, Cameron. We need to buy the flowers. For Daddy," she said. "Remember. We promised." Saying this, she could not remember there being any reason to feel such urgency. No reason to keep promises on a day she intended to leave him. Already, she was shaking the vicar's hand but had missed hearing his name.

"My son," she said, thrusting Cameron in front of her. "This is my son. Cameron. He admired your red door."

She immediately determined the vicar was an admirable man. Or perhaps it was pity she felt. He had a speech impediment. At first, she thought he was missing his teeth. But this was not the reason he skipped over those consonants. There were teeth, small and even and well kept. It was his lips that barely moved so what escaped was like water flowing. Sentences poured from his mouth. *What a plunge!* This vicar loved to talk. And with an urgency, like water that is rising.

Water imagery contributed to the rhythm, the weightlessness, of the novel *Mrs. Dalloway.* Michael Cunningham acknowledged this in writing *The Hours*—a book that negated all Annie's dreams and ambitions to rewrite the story of Mrs. Dalloway and place Virginia's unforgettable character in modern times. Michael Cunningham had done it all and better than she could have ever imagined. The book was so brilliant it was made into an Oscar winning movie. Annie loved that movie. It involved a young woman—a mother with a young son, like herself—who escaped to a hotel simply to have time alone to read that novel by Virginia Woolf. And as that woman lay down the length of the bed, the room filled with water. Only in the woman's mind of course. To Virginia, that water had been symbolic of release. The author later drowned herself, filling her pockets with stones before entering a river not far from her house. Her husband, left behind. This just after the breakfast hour, was it not?

The vicar continued to speak, the words flowing so quickly Annie lost their meaning. *The war.* She heard him say this more than once. And, *My boys.*

"My boys," he was saying now. "All over the world, they are. Not just the Irish. But Russian. Polish. Even German. I prayed for them all. *With* them all. Too many died in my arms. I wrote their mothers. Died with a prayer on their lips, I said. But never did I mention confession. The Lord doesn't need to hear what he already knows. I still receive letters from a few of those boys. The ones who made it home. Men, of course, they are now. Old men like me. Men that went on to raise their own sons. Not me. I had me hundreds of sons. My boys. All over the world they are now. I was a father times they needed one most."

He was shaking his head. Annie's thoughts moved past him and onto *Mrs. Dalloway*. In that novel, a boy goes to war to return less than a man. Poor Septimus is described as merely a shadow of what a man's supposed to be. Shell shock. It was Michael Cunningham who suggested in *The Hours* that Virginia did not know it would be Septimus who would die when she began her novel. He claimed she pondered several scenarios, even entertaining the thought death would come to Mrs. Dalloway instead, this the reason for beginning the book with the urgency of the hour passing, and the constant flow of traffic, pedestrians asserting their need to get somewhere. Anywhere. And from what? Poor Mrs. Dalloway would never know. After all, she is like a fish swimming in too shallow waters. *What a lark!* But it is not for Mrs. Dalloway the hour tolls. It is Septimus, a shattered soul, who chooses to fly rather than fight the demons that haunt him. And so, out the window he goes.

"A good listener," the vicar was saying. "You're very kind. A beautiful young woman like yourself. There must be so many things you could be doing. Instead, you're here, listening to this old man tell his stories. I really shouldn't take much more of your time. I could keep you here all day. You and the boy. What a polite young man he is. I'll just tell you one more story. This told to me in a letter I received—oh, I don't know how many years ago now. It was like that then. Towards the end of the war. Whole families displaced. The Polish brought in, changing the character of entire towns. It's really three stories. But I know only one. The boy was at war so couldn't have known what it was like for his family. And the Polish folks—I'm sure they have their own story to tell. I only know how the boy reacted years later, when he was a man, and went back to see what was once his family home. Polish names on all the businesses. But inside—"

Michael Cunningham wove three stories into *The Hours* to justly rewrite and yet capture the essence of *Mrs. Dalloway*. He felt compelled to tell Virginia's story—from the writing of *Mrs. Dalloway* until the morning Virginia filled her pockets with stones and walked into a river. His second story described a contemporary Mrs. Dalloway who shops for flowers in planning a party to honor a man who will, in fact, choose to fall from a window.

It is the third story that affected Annie the most. In this story, a woman takes a room in a hotel to escape her life and experiences, in reading the novel *Mrs. Dalloway*, thoughts of drowning. And what has driven her to this? A stifling marriage and a life of seemingly no purpose. Shallow waters to wade in. A life, one might say, that is a lark.

"Not a one of the family portraits moved. All across the walls they were. This Polish family—never taking them down. And my boy—a man now but a boy when he was off to war and his family displaced so the Polish could be given homes. You can imagine. He just stood their tongue-tied. Couldn't ask what possessed them. He just turned and walked away. Never been back."

"An amazing story," Annie said. But she had heard hardly a word except for the end. And this made little sense to her now. Was the returning soldier German? Russian? She could not ask without appearing rude. She reached into her purse and pulled out a card. "My husband's a journalist," she said. "He'd love to hear that story. May I ask him to come find you? Here? No. You keep his card. Please. That way you'll know who he is when he comes by."

She pressed the card into the vicar's hand knowing now exactly what she would do and how important was this single act. "Is there a bathroom I could use?" she asked.

He motioned down the hall. "On your right. Don't go left. It'll put you back on the street."

"If you'll excuse me then. You'll watch my son?"

"I'll show him the windows. I used to teach little boys. There was a school here once. Just the other side of that wall."

Already, the vicar was holding Cameron's hand.

Annie walked down the hall and turned to the right. She looked back but the vicar had already led her son from the foyer and so, her sight. But then again, she had known since the moment she woke up that she would leave him.

She really had no choice. It was ten years to the very day. While never did an anniversary pass that she did not find some way to punish herself. It had begun as a lark (not yet did she think in those words, only sixteen, though already she had read *Mrs. Dalloway*). Sixteen years old and the parents out of town. No one to notice she borrowed the car. And the distance to school so short that Friday morning with so much on her mind. Because, like Mrs. Dalloway, she was planning a party.

How many times had she traveled that route before with her father? Up through the residential blocks and past the grammar school, the high school less than a quarter mile away. So much on her mind she reacted too late to the child— a boy, only six years old—who stepped out onto the crosswalk. He had flown, landing twenty feet away.

"What right," his mother said, years later, running into her at the drugstore, "have you ever to feel happiness again?"

Not that a moment in Annie's life had since ever passed quickly. There were years of court battles. And even before they were over, she jumped from her dormitory window. Then married. Had a son.

No. She did not deserve such happiness.

It had hit her, on seeing *The Hours*, what she would do. Like the woman who dreamed of drowning in a hotel room but instead, simply walked away—left one life behind in pursuit of another. Not that the life the woman gained was a good one. It was simply the life she deserved.

Annie was walking swiftly and with purpose. Where would she go? Did it matter? She had her passport. She could go anywhere. Anywhere Cameron would not wake at night to hear her scream from dreams of drowning. Anywhere Josh would not see her looking out a window longingly, closing it even as she thought, "What a lark. And today. Perhaps this is my day to fly."

THE CONTRIBUTORS

The Editor

John Tullius is the Founder and Director of The Maui Writers Conference.☐ He has written 15 books including coauthoring the bestsellers *Body of a Crime* and *Against the Law.*☐ He has also written scores of articles for dozens of magazines including *Cosmopolitan*, *Playboy* and *Town and Country*, and was a contributing editor at *Tennis Magazine*.

The Contributors

Lisa Alber has three completed novels and is currently plotting her way toward landing an agent. "Eileen and the Rock" is her second published story. In various incarnations, she has worked as a financial analyst in South America, editorial assistant in a major New York publishing house, cocktail waitress, journalist, and technical writer. She lives in Portland, Oregon.

Stacy Allen and her husband Ron have recently relocated to north Atlanta from Seattle. She has completed three novels, and is currently writing another. Her passions include global travel, foreign languages, cooking, reading, SCUBA diving, history, calligraphy and illumination, photography, and music. She writes full time. Her short story, "A King's Ransom," appeared in *Ship's Log: Writings At Sea* (TripleTree Publishing). Please visit her website at for more information.

Self-described as a pixie and still wondering what she will be when (if) she grows up, **Ardith Ashton** spends her time being retired. She travels a bit, which she loves, and putters around her Seaside, Oregon home. Born in Colorado, raised in Southern California, and finally finding her home in Oregon, her varied background includes retail clerking, secretarial duties at a major Oregon University, and mothering her three children, the most important people in her world.

Terry Brooks was born in Sterling, Illinois, in 1944. He received his undergraduate degree from Hamilton College, where he majored in English Literature, and his graduate degree from the School of Law at Washington & Lee University. A writer since the age of ten, he published his first novel, *The Sword of Shannara,* in 1977. It became the first work of fiction ever to appear on the New York Times Trade Paperback Bestseller List, where it remained for over five months. He has written twenty-two novels, two movie adaptations, and a memoir on his writing life. He has sold over twenty-five million copies of his books and is published worldwide. He lives with his wife Judine in the Pacific Northwest and Hawaii.

Dani Brown earned a bachelor degree of science in nursing. Married to a physician, Ms Brown is currently retired from nursing to raise their four children and focus on her writing career. She is a member of the state medical alliance board and enjoys travel, reading and community service.

Carolyn Buchanan lives in Auburn, Alabama with her husband, Jerry. They have two sons, Bill and B.G. She has an MFA in Creative Writing from Antioch University at Los Angeles. This is her third Maui Writers' Challenge.

Aimée Carter has been writing for most of her twenty years, starting off with fan fiction and then branching off into original novel-length fiction. With more than a dozen manuscripts under her belt, she is currently a student at the University of Michigan, majoring in Political Science.

Art and psychology combined have driven an unusual combination of careers, acquaintances, and experiences that have led **Bonnie Christoffersen** to become a writer. A current resident of Bainbridge Island, Washington, she has moved from one beach community to the next before settling on a harbor with her husband and two children.

Lucie Barron Eggleston, founder and president of Letter-Perfect Communications, has written two books on business writing. In 2005, she co-authored *Create Your Own Family Originals* to inspire others to celebrate their stories. Born in the second month of the Baby Boom, Lucie now lives in Columbia, South Carolina with her husband Bob and their yellow lab, Hollywood.

Jerry Eiting is a Maui-based Baritone with a B.F.A. in Musical Theater from U.S.I.U. in San Diego. He is owner of Prime Time, a publication focusing on senior living on Maui, and co-owner of Maui Party Lights, specializing in tropical lighting for weddings and parties on the island.

Elizabeth Engstrom has written nine books and over two hundred fifty short stories, articles and essays. She is a sought-after instructor, lecturer and keynote speaker at writing conferences and conventions around the world. She was an initial faculty member of the Maui Writers Conference, and served as the Director of the Maui Writers Retreat for a decade. She is currently a regular contributor to Court TV.

Many things are changing in **Val Ford's** life. Non-writing work comes and goes, two of her three children are grown, and the Labradors are aging. But she still has green eyes and a good man. Val & Bill & Tony live in the forest outside Springfield, Oregon.

Elizabeth George is the New York Times and internationally best selling author of a series of crime novels set in Great Britain. She is also the author of the bestselling writers' guide *Write Away* as well as the editor of *A Moment on the Edge,* an anthology of crime stories by women in the 20th century. She is a longtime instructor of creative writing and a former high school English teacher.

Gail Harris has recently retired after twenty-eight years of working for the government and three years in corporate America. She is currently living happily ever after in Durango, Colorado.

As a child, **Judith Heath** breathed the ember of her spirit to life reading under the covers with a flashlight; taking oxygen from tales of imperfect heroes who overcame dragons and wicked stepmothers. Later, with her sons, she left gnome cakes at the verge of twilight woods, taking the empty plate at dawn as proof of offerings received. She lives in Hawaii where she has completed her first fantasy novel.

Christopher Keane has written fifteen books that have sold in the millions, in forty-three languages worldwide. He's written movies from his books and other sources, produced at major studios. His *The Huntress* was a hit TV series on USA. He's just finished a true-life political thriller about JFK and his greatest love, Mary Meyer, whose influence inadvertently led to his assassination and to her own. His first book, *The Hunter*, was made into Steve McQueen's last movie of the same name. He's writing a novel about a strange New Hampshire lakeside town and the odd people who live there—just down the road from a farm where he and his wife, Susan Crawford, spend part of their time. He teaches and lectures in Boston and Cambridge, at Emerson and Harvard. □

Judith G. Lyeth, Judie to her friends, has followed an eclectic path to realizing her dream of becoming a writer. An anthropology degree in college and twenty years in the travel business have given her lots of material for stories. She lives in Castle Rock, Colorado with her cat, Arkaelian, and a resident wizard.

Mike Malaghan, author of *Making Millions in Direct Sales* (McGraw Hill, 2005), is directing his post-corporate career writing to two novels. One shows how white supremacists plan to use video game violence to program teenagers to kill black leaders. The second novel, taking advantage of Mike's travels to more than 100 countries, uses the pearl industry as a backdrop to one man's consequences in choosing loyalty instead of his personal values.

David Nutt, living quietly in Paris, writes for a French cheese website which he co- founded, Fromages.com. He is trying his hand at writing short stories and poetry. The current project on the drawing board—more appropriately stated would be on the writing board—is a poetry book: a romantic view of thirty well-known French cheeses with artistic (drawings and photographs) illustrations. Included will be three short stories about cheese and a few succulent recipes. The trip to Ireland was a joy and a great intellectual stimulus for writing interesting short stories. Now for the execution!

Richard Ramsey's days are filled with the hum of computers and bright workstation screens while his nights overflow with forgotten magic, druids, and failing fairy knots. Between these worlds lie the Pacific Northwest, his wife, and three cats. Though returning to the present has its dangers, living in the ancient past would be without the support and caring of his wife. His anchor is here, but his memories are from there.

With this piece, **Myrtle Forberg Siebert** begins experimenting with fiction. Her non-fiction includes high school texts in foods and nutrition, and a personalized family history. The latter details the life of her grandfather, his immigration to North America from Norway, and the lives of his descendents in the Pacific Northwest.

Dr. Margaret Stratton started making things up thirty years ago to entertain her children. They had dragons in the car engine, fairies and elves in the glove box, and a strong young prince saving his father's kingdom. She took a brief shot at a writing class and had some poetry published as a result, but detoured after that and focused on studying for what she thought to be a 'proper career' as a clinical psychologist. Now she has a full time day job as a licensed psychologist and hopes to follow Terry Brooks' example and have several books published and a year's salary in the bank before she makes the transition to full time fiction writing.

Heather Varez lives with her husband, three children, cats, chickens, and dogs in a fern forest on the Big Island of Hawaii. In a home they built, overlooking the massive brothers of Mauna Loa and Mauna Kea, she writes primarily romance.

Margaret Zacharias has published feature articles and short stories as well as art, theater, music, and literary reviews. She writes and performs for Salisbury House & Gardens Foundation, DMWC at Hoyt Sherman Place Theater, and the Catholic Diocese of Des Moines, Iowa.

The Maui Writers Conference takes place during Labor
Day weekend every year.
For more information, contact:

The Maui Writers Conference
PO Box 1118
Kihei, Maui, Hawaii 86753
808-879-0061
www.mauiwriters.com